The Heart of England

The Heart of England

by

HONOR TRACY

HAMISH HAMILTON

London

First published in Great Britain 1983
by Hamish Hamilton Ltd
Garden House 57–59 Long Acre London WC2E 9JZ

British Library Cataloguing in Publication Data

Tracy, Honor
  The heart of England.
  1. West Country (England) – Description and travel
  I. Title
  914.23'04858   DA670.W4
  ISBN 0-241-10339-8

Typeset by Computape (Pickering) Ltd
Printed and bound in Great Britain
at the Pitman Press, Bath

To Richard Bennett

Acknowledgements

Among the many people who helped me collect the material for this book, I should like to thank Canon Vanstone of Chester Cathedral, for giving me so much of his time: Dr Hunt, of Worcester Cathedral, for explaining the musical arrangements there: Mr and Mrs Robin Farquhar-Oliver, Miss June Grimble and Miss Margaret Boldry, for much hospitality: Miss June Hebden, Librarian of Malvern Public Library, and Mrs Firth and Mrs Clist, Honorary Librarians of the Hanley Swan Branch, for kindly help and forbearance.

I also wish to remember my dear friend and colleague, the late 'Bunty' Arrowsmith, Hanley Swan correspondent of *Berrow's Journal*, Worcester, who was a mine of information, a most lively companion and the best of friends in need.

Chapter One

G. K. Chesterton was called on once by a friend at his Battersea home and found to be busy packing. The friend asked where he was off to, and he replied: To Battersea. This paradoxical remark was later made the introduction to an essay on the joys of rediscovery. G.K. was simply going abroad for a spell so that his beloved habitat would glow with a fresh lustre on his return.

This evening I too was packing up in my cottage by the sea on Achill Island in Mayo, and I too was bent on rediscovery, not of Achill however but of my native England. Since the war I had been so much away that it had almost become 'abroad'. My brief visits were usually to London where the continual transformation was such that often I hardly knew where I was, even in quarters which once I had known intimately. Some of the changes were not bad, others were frightful, but together they turned it into a foreign city, with only a few little enclaves preserved here and there. As for the country parts I knew best, many of them were unrecognizable: one of the pleasant little towns near my childhood home had broken out in a rash of factories, employing thousands of immigrants, half black, half Irish: and a charming inn I remembered there was said to be the headquarters of the local IRA.

And so I had decided to go in search of an England which for me was the real, the only, one; and here I now was, packing away like mad under the critical eye of Polly, my small Irish hunt terrier, who understood perfectly what I was up to. The battered old suitcase into which items were methodically put then fretfully tossed out again, the slummy aspect of the room, the familiar display of bemused incompetence, all signified that her globe- trotting mistress – though 'mistress' is a misnomer – was off again. She herself would go happily to the house of some dear friends, with as play-mate a red setter who adored her and whom she ruled with a paw of iron: no need there to sit quiet by the hour while I scribbled or typed. Nevertheless, she had not been consulted and was making her displeasure felt.

And such was her innate shrewdness and so severe her mien that I almost fancied she had divined that I was going where no restrictions were put on dogs coming from here. Why am I not invited? she seemed to be thinking: I am badly in need of a change myself. But I hardly knew as yet which way I should take, or what I was in for, in what kind of hotels or inns I should be staying. I wanted to visit cathedrals, museums and other buildings where she would not be wel-come. I wanted to talk to many kinds of people, and she had a deplorable habit, inherited from her snob of a mother: if she didn't like a person's looks, she nipped him smartly on the ankle. No, there was nothing doing; and she sat there with her sulks until the sound of our friends' car at the door brought an outburst of joyful barks and I was at once forgot-ten. I completed my preparations in peace and in due course set off for Dublin, Dun Laoghaire and the night boat to Holyhead.

Chapter Two

I set off for England by way of the Irish mailboat, tossing up and down on a choppy sea and travelling for all my first-class ticket in second-class conditions. The Irish prole regards the fact of there being a first class as an insult and a challenge, if not an infringement of his Human Rights. It does not appear to cross his mind that it is a simple matter of what you pay. To prove himself as good as the next he marches firmly into First, thereby transforming it immediately into Second; and, poor working-man, unable to afford the difference in fare, proceeds to spend six times the amount at the bar. Feeble attempts by a steward to prevent it happening are, as a rule, soon given up.

The question arises every time of where to sit. In a non-smoking lounge there will be harassed mothers and screaming children and a multitude of brown paper parcels. If you prefer even the stench of stale cheap tobacco, there are the bars with their reeling shouting patrons, their serried ranks of dirty glasses, their pools of stout on table and floor, glinting under the lights like the pools of a bog. Whichever you choose, you will probably wish you had chosen the other; and once you are settled, it is unwise to move as the boat invariably seems to be full, whatever the time of year, you have lost your place and will not find another.

If it is better than Heathrow, it is only because anything must be. Had Cardinal Hume become Pope, I cannot imagine him falling down and kissing the tarmac there, as John Paul II kissed the earth on arriving in Poland. Indeed, I cannot imagine Heathrow inspiring any emotion whatever, except perhaps a homicidal frenzy.

But the crossing is only three and a half hours and I am a good sailor. Now the lights of Holyhead began to twinkle on the horizon, presently we were drawing alongside the quay, loudspeakers gave a last warning to beware of pick-pockets and urged the feckless to look for their straying progeny. The passengers, migrant workers and their families, many of whom had come from the ends of Ireland that same day, wearily lined up for the Customs, police and the long haul to Euston. They would arrive in that station, once so welcoming and now rebuilt to resemble a stockyard as closely as could be, between five and six in the morning and with luck might get a cardboard beaker of tasteless coffee or tea.

I was only going as far as Chester, and on English trains first-class tickets are still honoured, so that I was much better off. Before I boarded the train, however, there was likely to be some little to-do with a porter. Except for a walking tour in my youth I have never visited Wales; but if the porters at Holyhead are typical of her inhabitants, it would be a powerful argument in favour of devolution. A more prickly and crossgrained bunch I don't think I ever found.

Sure enough, one of them tore past me with a loaded trolley which cannoned against my own heavy case and all but knocked me down. I called after him to mind how he went, at which he instantly left his trolley to bowl along by itself and returned to give me a piece of his mind.

'You are telling me how to do my job, isn't it?' he shouted in his singsong. 'That is good. I am to be taught my job, which I have done for thirty years. Besides having fought in the war with distinction. In my opinion of it, woman, you are intoxicated!'

With that he sprinted after his trolley and, overtaking it, resumed his Panzer-like charge through the milling crowds. It might well take thirty years or so to acquire that technique, I reflected, and also to comment on critics with such lucidity.

Tired as I was, it gave me a pleasant thrill when the train drew up and I saw CHESTER marked in the all but deserted station. I had been through the city dozens of times but never got out there, always meaning to do so 'one of these days'. There were no porters about, nor even a guard or a ticket collector to be seen, although one or two lights were burning in the offices still. I picked up my bag and went out to the quiet empty street, which looked unnaturally clean after the profuse litter of Dublin. It was the first thing really to strike

4

me since landing, and it was odd because I had seen so many lamentations in the newspapers about the filthy state of England now. Probably they meant London, which is hardly England any longer.

I had not booked a room because it was only April. But the large hotel near the station was full and the night porter assured me that it was necessary to book everywhere nowadays, whatever the season. People were always on the move, he couldn't say why. He hoped I would be lucky but doubted it. Still, it was after three o'clock, in a few hours people would start getting up and some would be leaving, so all I would have to do would be to hang about until a room fell free.

The prospect of tramping about an unfamiliar city in the cold and wet was gloomy enough even without a bag which suddenly felt as if stuffed with iron bars; but it soon turned out that the porter had merely been indulging a taste for woe and disaster, and a room was available at the next hotel some fifty yards away.

One has to be careful with generalizations because very often they are no sooner uttered than all the exceptions come crowding in. Nevertheless, it does seem to me that the English are the slowest, most reluctant, to welcome a stranger of any people I know. Of Turks, Afghans, the Jivaro Indians of Ecuador and others said to be of a rebarbative disposition, I cannot speak, having no experience of them; but the radiant Italian smile, the grave Spanish courtesy, the suave if commercial *accueil* of the French, the Austrian *Gemütlichkeit*, will hardly be found here.

The night porter at the second hotel turned over the pages of his register, frowning much as a policeman might while he looked for a vacant cell. Presently he said 'Number Nineteen' in a sepulchral voice and passed me the key without another word. He seemed taken aback that anyone arriving at three-thirty a.m. should want breakfast in bed, and positively shocked when I asked if someone would take my suitcase for me; however, he glumly agreed to both, which was fortunate as regarded my bag, for this big and by no means cheap establishment did not run to a lift. The room was spotless and my breakfast appeared in the morning dead on time – brought by a maid with martyrdom in every line of her face.

Thus an aura of disapproval seemed to hover about me which I had done nothing to deserve. Visitors to this hotel were apparently guilty of something or other until they had proved themselves innocent. But when I had dressed and gone downstairs I found everyone smiling and disposed to be agreeable. Now the attitude appeared to be, Well, we made every attempt to frighten this woman off but here she still is, so let us make the best of it.

Saturday forenoon was not the happiest time to make Chester's acquaintance. The fine patrician streets were bursting with proles of every age and size, the younger mostly licking ice-creams or munching things out of paper bags. For some years past on my trips to London I had noted how many fat young males there were, some with an alderman's belly while still in their teens; but as it often went with a sallow skin, mandarin-type moustache or other exotic trait, I thought perhaps they belonged to a race which prized obesity. This was a purely English lot, however, and the Billy Bunters were every bit as plentiful. There were almost as many Bessies too, which I had not seen in London. With them it showed more in the face: one that stood out was as round and shiny and red as a giant tomato with what seemed to be two black currants stuck in it but must have been eyes, the whole surmounted by an Afro frizz of carroty hair. I had not been walking for twenty minutes before I caught sight of a youth literally wedged in a doorway. It will be interesting to watch how things develop, particularly as domestic building and furniture have tended for a long while now to get smaller and skimpier.

I drifted along with the noisy cheerful mob, it being impossible to move at a normal pace, noting places of interest to return to at a quieter hour and much admiring the shops. Apart from the ubiquitous chain stores, these had a style very much of their own, elegant and earthy at once, and delightfully old-fashioned. There were the long established gun-smiths and saddlers with their tweedy weather-beaten customers, people whose family had probably dealt here for generations. In some of the former, sign of the times, there

6

might be an assortment of daggers and flick knives, the mere possession of which, I have been told, is an offence today. There were endless bakeries of inviting appearance with their crusty loaves and fruity cakes: chemists with soaps, scents and lotions of a time gone by: handsewn boots and shoes, antiques, porcelain and souvenir knick-knacks that one would not be ashamed to buy. The very chain stores seemed lightly touched by grace, even Woolworth's not so entirely itself as elsewhere.

Many of them are in the famous Rows, which consist of a double tier, ground level and first floor, the upper set a little way back, leaving room for a promenade and reached by stairs at regular intervals. There are balconies all along this on which one can lean and contemplate the passersby below, that most delightful of occupations. The Rows are one of the distinctive features of the city, which claims that they are unique; and certainly I have seen nothing like them before. In the Middle Ages, shops of a kind would huddle together, so that there was Fishmongers' Row, the Kynge Fysshe Borde, the Butter shops and Milk Stoups, Cooks' Row, Pepper Alley and so on; and the Guide mentions one suggestively named Broken-Shin Row, in tribute to the quality of its paving. All that has long since gone, however, and now they are all jumbled up, textiles, buns, antiques, books.

Particularly charming in this city of whitewashed black-timbered houses were the flowers everywhere at this moment, disposed in tubs about the streets and squares or massed in parks and open spaces, hyacinths, tulips, daffodils, many of new shapes and colours. I took this to be a normal amenity until, passing the City Hall, I saw the Dutch flag fluttering from the staff outside it. Thinking we must have been quietly invaded and occupied, I went into the Hall itself to inquire of the Mayor, or Burgomeester now perhaps, and learned that in honour of Chester's eleventh centenary the Dutch had sent thousand upon thousand of their beautiful bulbs; and these being now in bloom and the city full of Dutch visitors, their flag was raised as a mark of esteem and gratitude. In the thirteenth and fourteenth centuries, when Chester was one of the busiest ports, there was much trading with Holland and a Dutch influence is seen in many of the

7

buildings there today; and to remember this now, when Chester is a port no longer, was a kindly imaginative act indeed, to be rewarded, let us hope, with streams of orders for the generous bulb men.

The Dutch had come over on purpose to see the display and were mainly growers or journalists. The general foreign influx had not yet begun, and I reckoned we should be safe from it for some time, as it was very cold for the time of year. It was good to see this fine old town in her everyday dress, which included items that in many places might have been put on as a treat for tourists.

Among them was the Town Crier, described by himself as the World Champion in that line, though I should have thought he was about the only one. The last I came across was in Southwold, Suffolk, when I was a very small girl and the Crier, a portly old gentleman with white whiskers, coming up to his retirement and not to be replaced. With immense dignity he paced the quiet streets of that little seaside borough, pausing at four or five different points to ring his bell and declaim 'Oyez! Oyez! Oyez!' (which I understood as Oh Yes! and never could make head or tail of) and bawl out the local news.

This specimen was very different, although dressed in the same eighteenth-century fashion, scarlet cloak and shoulder cape, black cocked hat, knee breeches and buckled shoes. He was much younger and sported a pigtail of his own dark hair, and he looked round his audience with a sly twinkle in his small brown eyes. It is said that he has the loudest voice in England, and it certainly does carry. Twice daily throughout the year, at noon and three o'clock, he stands at the City Cross where the Watergate, Bridge, Eastgate and Northgate streets intersect and, instead of news, announces entertainments and sport or recommends shops and restaurants.

He also has a line in pawky *sotto voce* for the delectation of those nearest his stand: '(ff) at ******* you will find the GREATEST AMERICAN DISASTER (PP) and I don't mean Mr Nixon (ff) the HAM- or BEEFBURGER!' If any of what seems to be a regular following presumes to interrupt or heckle he rounds on them: 'Now then, I'm *paid* to make a fool of myself. What's your excuse?' Finally he roars 'God Save the Queen! God Save the Earl of Chester (i.e. the Prince of Wales)! God Save the Mayor!' and marches back to base in the British Heritage headquarters.

After enjoying his midday performance I began to think about luncheon and strolled about until I should find a place that took my fancy. With a beginner's luck I came on one behind the Cathedral, where you went through an old courtyard to a restaurant on the ground floor and a buffet upstairs with many delicious kinds of salad and cold meat, with real mayonnaise what was more, not the infamous 'cream' that comes out of a bottle.

Here something rather funny occurred, although it did not amuse me at the time. I had bought a newspaper to see how the general election campaign was going and put it and my briefcase on a chair at a table for two before lining up at the snack bar. Ahead of me were two middle-aged women with striking hats and striking voices; and what was my surprise on returning to this table to find them in possession of it and my belongings dumped on the floor beside. There was no excuse for this act of piracy because the room was barely half full, but when I mildly pointed out that one place here was bespoken, they both set about me. There was no reserving in this buffet, it wasn't allowed, against the rules, not done . . .

Would they, then, I asked still mildly, be good enough to pass my things?

'Oh. These are yours, are they?' They were fished up and thrust at me.

'Extraordinary behaviour,' I murmured.

'That's what we think!' barked one of the buccaneers.

They were a species of female Tory dragon, plentiful in my youth, which I rather supposed would have died out by now; but not a bit of it. These two at any rate had come through the levelling postwar years in triumph, without a scale knocked off them. The odd thing was, the Labour propaganda machine was making an ass of itself just then with fantasies about The Honourable Algernon, the like of which never existed but in their own fervent brains, while here was stark reality, theirs for the taking. Either of these women, if faithfully depicted, could have done them no end of good whereas Algernon was merely a giggle. Two young people, the man bearded, the girl kaftan'd, made room for me at the next table, broadly smiling. They had Guardian Reader written all over them but on this point at least we were as one.

I spoke of beginner's luck in finding this excellent place with the excellent food and wine and moderate prices, but I was shortly to find out that Chester abounds in good eating houses. Nearly all of them were English, too, and the only dire meal I had during my stay was when some icy weather induced me not to leave the hotel. Anyone fool enough to eat in a provincial English hotel, for whatever reason, deserves no sympathy. As I remember it, there was a choice of prawn cocktail or Brown Windsor soup – this nation seems hooked on Brown Windsor soup – grey roast beef with soggy Yorkshire pudding and tinned peas and Trifle, which left a haunting flavour of hair-oil behind it. I saw but one Indian and one Chinese restaurant, and in fact the whole city was amazingly free of the oriental presence. Friends of mine afterwards told me how once they were about to enter the Indian place when a workman called out urgently, advising them against it. There was a good Wimpy's not far away, he said, 'and this – why, it's Continental, for a start!'

I spent the afternoon wandering about and gazing in utter bliss. Why on earth had I never come here before? I had expected much, but not as much: I was quite bowled over, as when I first saw Oxford. Those lovely timbered buildings in Watergate Street, with such endearing names as Refuge House, or mottoes, as Providence is my Inheritance. That a busy unromantic commercial life went on behind the façade made no difference. And as evening came on, the sun sinking in a pale green sky, I had a long memorable walk on the Roman wall that embraces the inner city, high above it, with views over the Roman ruins, the river, churches, parks and now and then some faraway hills.

It was not a place to tire of easily either. Even the peripatetic Boswell thought that here he might conceivably settle down. 'I was quite enchanted at Chester, so that I could hardly quit it,' he wrote to Johnson, promising to send a copy of the journal he had kept, 'Which is truly a log-book of felicity.' This drew a douche of cold water from the Grand Cham, who would not have him 'exalt your pleasures ...

beyond their real state. Why should you not be as happy at Edinburgh as at Chester?' But Johnson himself had one of his rare disagreements with Mrs Thrale for keeping her daughter out too long on the city wall, so that this remarkably foolish question may have been due to spleen.

The city proper is small, and unless you were born within the ramparts you do not truly belong. Those ramparts are to the people of Chester what Bow Bells are to the Cockney. Everyone born outside is a foreigner. And nowadays the business house congestion within is such that not many domestic areas remain. You see little that is new, mercifully enough, to judge from one exception, the Gateway Theatre, a contemporary box set in the city's heart. It prides itself on catering for every taste and, in addition to the classics, has a wide range of trendy London hits.

As the dinner hour came on, I returned to the courtyard near the Cathedral, keeping a sharp look-out for Tory ladies. In the evening the buffet is transformed into a bistro where for a fixed sum – (£4.25 then, goodness knows how much today) you could eat as much as you liked. 'Help yourself again and again', a friendly notice said. In the ordinary way it probably did very well with the abstemious English, who rarely have second helpings even at home; but tonight the place was thronged with gargantuan Dutch, who were trotting steadily back and forth to pile their plates anew, while the staff looked nervously on.

'I am afraid there is not much left,' the manageress ruefully informed me as I produced my entry ticket; and indeed, one did get the impression of an army of locusts having passed that way. Still, at least they were Dutch and not Germans, who under those conditions would be likely to scoop whatever remained into plastic bags and carry it off, on the grounds that it was paid for.

At the hotel I decided on a nightcap and early bed, but ran into difficulties here as well. There were two bars, one with a jukebox going full tilt, and the other full of red-faced amateur politicians, bawling for a dictatorship. Accordingly I skipped that part of the programme and went upstairs; but no sooner did my head touch the pillow than a diabolical shindy broke out in the room directly beneath. It was a kind of unearthly howl, accompanied by a relentless beat on drums and other percussion instruments, as if some African freedom fighters were celebrating a massacre with an orgy: not at all what one would expect to find in a solid Edwardian hotel, rife with gilt, mahogany, mirrors and deep red carpets.

As it kept up, after half an hour or so I rang the reception desk and asked what was going on. Apparently, it was a teenagers' disco, supposed to shut at eleven but apt to continue into the small hours at the week-end.

'We've had complaints about it,' said the night porter, he of the forbidding aspect the night before, 'but there, you know how it is. No use our talking to *them*. Would you like another room? There's plenty going.'

Then why have stuck me immediately above this raging inferno? It looked like persecution. But the night porter himself came up and in the most amiable manner escorted me to an upper floor, promising that my luggage should follow first thing in the morning. True enough, the rooms all round seemed to be uninhabited. A profound and blessed peace reigned everywhere. The whole thing was as strange as could be, but I was too sleepy to think about it then. I woke next morning, to find the sun streaming in through the windows and the martyred woman of yesterday standing beside my bed with my breakfast tray in her hands and a motherly smile on her lips. Having failed to scare me off, the hotel staff was evidently willing to make the best of a bad job and relax.

Chapter Three

The people of Chester are inclined to be on the defensive about their Cathedral. It is something of a hotchpotch and the colour of its walls may be described as puce. But it has an interesting history of ups and downs as some well- preserved remains bear witness. In the early tenth century a church was built on the site as a burial ground for St Werburgh, a Mercian princess who had been active in setting up monasteries in the country roundabout. Throughout the Middle Ages her shrine was venerated by pilgrims, but the Conquest put paid to that, as to so much else.

In 1093 a Norman, Hugh Lupus, Earl of Chester, transformed it into a Benedictine monastery, rich and powerful, surrounded by fair broad acres and so it continued for five centuries until Henry VIII dissolved it in 1540, pocketing much of its wealth. It was then made a Cathedral, given a bishop (a crony of the Monarch) and re-dedicated to Christ and the Virgin Mary. But although the Order was driven out, their habitations survived to a remarkable degree. There are the cloisters with the recesses or open cells in which the monks sat reading or writing, the cloister garden, still beautifully kept, the chapter house where the community met to discuss matters of discipline or organization, the refectory with a pulpit built up in the wall from which a monk would read an edifying work at meal-times, the parlour for the reception of non- Benedictine visitors and the crypt, all added at different times, no doubt as funds were available. What is missing today is the growl of monks chanting the Office, the stream of callers, suppliant or penitent, and the special atmosphere of peace and activity that hangs about a Benedictine foundation.

Evensong in an Anglican cathedral is a pleasure that I had not enjoyed for many years. The grace, precision and beauty of it were all but forgotten and I felt carried away, as I had been by the city itself. And the care that had obviously been lavished on the place suggested an army of willing unpaid workers. There were no dead flowers or grubby surplices, no dull brasses or coats of dust, no tipsily reeling candles. Could it have been the doing of female hands? If so, it is pleasant to think that after all the churches have some use for women, apart from providing the bulk of the congregation.

Here, even the choir sopranos were girls, 'standing in' for the boys who had been given a holiday after their Easter exertions. This was explained to me afterwards by one of the clergy with a slight air of deprecation as if he were apologizing for a makeshift. He need not have done so for me, as the gentle sweetness of the girlish voices was very much to my liking. It is true that those of boys are colder and sharper, not to say piercing, but why these qualities should be thought so desirable is more than I can imagine. This was Evensong, moreover; and I never can hear males singing the Magnificat without an unseemly desire to laugh.

Best of all, better than even the ambience and the music and the sound of English properly spoken, was the Cathedral's using the Book of Common Prayer and the Authorized Version of the Bible. Heaven knows, the new English rite forced upon us Catholics is dreadful enough, but we have been conditioned to believe that docility, no matter in respect of what, is a virtue in itself. As regards our separated brethren, however, one might have expected more spirit. I have always assumed that the Reformation in England came about not through the king's divorce or about points of doctrine but because our sturdy people were tired of being ordered about by foreigners. Yet here they are today, with these priceless treasures to draw on, produced when our language was at the height of its beauty and power, tamely consenting to throw them aside for a crude and feeble substitute that all too successfully apes the speech of the common man.

But not apparently in the splendid Cathedral of Chester. I felt that here and now was the start of my journey, one purpose of which was to look for England under all the trash that had been dumped on her lovely face since the war. And

14

apart from the invigorating rhythms of the ancient prose, a frankly English note was struck throughout. Yesterday had been the birthday of the Queen, tomorrow would be the Feast of St George – demoted by an Italian Pope, to be sure, but a fig for that – and so we went lustily to work singing to, and praying for, our country. It did seem an auspicious beginning.

After the service, as the people went out, I saw a clergyman standing near the door and greeting various of the regulars that he knew. A long time ago I worked as a newspaper correspondent and was often having to buttonhole strangers, whether they liked it or not, and it left me very unwilling to do so since. Should I, could I, bring myself to speak to this man? On the whole I thought not. But then, taking courage from his friendly air, I went up and asked if some one of the Cathedral might be able to spare me a few minutes on the following day. It was well for me that my scruples were overcome, for he promptly asked me to tea and our subsequent few meetings are among the pleasantest memories of my stay.

He was a man of about sixty with an open good-humoured face and a look that was both shrewd and reflective. And it was clear at once that he had a real sense of humour and could be depended on not to tell any of those little clerical jokes. He lived in Abbey Square, a peaceful enclosure to be entered through an arch: at night, a pole descends across the road and is padlocked, only residents having a key. It would be an attractive place at any time with the pretty houses, the flower gardens and well-kept grass but now with the yellow forsythia blooming all round it was enchanting. The Canon was ready with tea and cherry cake, the latter something else that I had all but forgotten, home made too as befitted a cathedral close.

Hearing that I had come from Ireland and had spent some time in Belfast, he asked about things there and for a while our talk was of that. A story told me by a social worker in the Ardoyne district pleased him mightily: it concerned an IRA man, a practising Catholic whom somebody asked how he squared his murders with his conscience, how he spoke of them at confession and what his confessor had to say.

15

'I don't confess them at all,' he gravely replied. 'Sure, what business is that of the priest?'

Solemn critics have so often rapped my knuckles for what they wrongly believe is levity on such matters, it did me good to hear the Canon's delighted laugh.

I told him how much the form of service had pleased me the afternoon before, and he said he thought there was a growing reaction against novelty for novelty's sake. This came chiefly from the younger clergy and when some of the senior men at the top had been removed, there would be hope again. I could well believe it. The supporters of our own New Mass and other innovations such as guitar playing and fanciful capers at the altar are mostly the middle-aged or elderly, scared of seeming dated or out of touch. He also informed me about the Cathedral and its history, some of what he said being at variance with the official guide, apt as guides so often are to confuse legend with fact. At a quarter past five he had an appointment, but at seven a colleague was to take a number of would-be guides on a conducted tour and he suggested that we join them.

I spent the intervening time in contrasting fashion at the Pied Bull, claimed to be the oldest tavern in Chester with a continuous history. My plan was merely to look around and wet my whistle, but a free entertainment, almost a cabaret, was provided by a woman who rushed in and poured out a torrent of abuse at the owner. Evidently it was not for the first time, as the owner stood there with the resigned expression of a man who has been here before. Exactly what her complaint was never emerged, but so rich was her vocabulary that a respectable lady remarked, when the intruder at last was gone, that she had never heard so many awful words in so short a time. This she said without a trace of censure but as one who mentions a simple, arresting fact, such as you find in the Guinness Book of Records.

It made me think of Bunyan's description of himself in his unregenerate days: 'I knew not how to speak, unless I put an oath before and another behind to make my words have authority.' And although the woman's hair was mousy and I had no idea as to her calling, somehow she put me in mind of Oliver Gogarty's 'Redheaded Whore of Ringsend', one of his finest poems and probably aimed at Ireland:

> And listen each night
> For her querulous shout
> As at last she streels in
> And the pubs empty out.
> To soothe that wild breast
> With my old fangled songs
> Till she feels it redressed
> From inordinate wrongs,
> Imagined, outrageous
> Preposterous wrongs
> Shall be all I will do ...

How true it is that variety is the spice of life! Between the urbanity of the Canon's tea and the informative tour of the Cathedral, the interlude with Doll Tearsheet in this ancient inn was a piquant change of note.

Back in the noble pile, I found the training guides assembled under the leadership of a cleric. They were of all sorts and sizes, masterful matrons, retired business men, dreamy-eyed enthusiasts of either sex and any age, a profusion of old dears and the Town Crier himself, in full fig but without his bell and bounce. I was too busy observing them all and wondering which I would choose if I had to to take in much of what was said; and besides, the Canon was there to give me some entertaining individual instruction.

The Choir was perhaps the most striking feature, with its fourteenth-century stalls, beautifully carved, among them a splendid Tree of Jesse, father of David, showing the descent of Jesus Christ. The Canon led me to a special favourite of his, the figure of a woman reading. No doubt the book in her hands was of an improving nature, but the smirk on her face suggested the contrary, as if she had come on the contemporary equivalent of a comic and sneaked off to enjoy it in safe seclusion beneath the canonical chair. I mentioned that in Spain the tip-up seats of the *coros* often had carvings of an inappropriate even a ribald, character on the

17

underside; and the Canon said that this was true of some of them here. One lurid specimen had latterly been replaced by a symbolical treatment of the United Nations.

Another of his favourites was a painting of the Trinity on one of the bosses in the Lady Chapel. Above was God the Father, staring before him with the impassive calm of the Pancrator in a Byzantine mosaic, and below the Son, spent, exhausted, dying on the cross with the Dove, or Holy Ghost, cooing at his ear; and this, to the Canon's mind, was a pure expression of the Divine Love. I may have garbled his explanation somewhat, and I may well have misjudged the painting itself, seeing it for the first time and most uncomfortably with my head tilted back at a right angle – why cannot stretchers on wheels be provided for the study of ceiling decoration – but it struck me as merely of its epoch. The blankness of the Father's face had no philosophical idea behind it, but was due to the fact that portrait painting, the manifestation of spirit through the external features, still lay in a distant future. Or so I thought then. Subsequently, I bought a book that the Canon had written, *Love's Endeavour, Love's Expense*, and found it full of bold and original ideas which helped me to understand his opinion rather better. I was also struck by another pensée of his, namely that the Creator possibly makes an occasional bosh shot, like any other artist. Whether this would appeal to an orthodox theologian I cannot say, but certainly, if true, it would account for a very great deal.

It was still on the early side for dinner when our tour was concluded and I gave myself the treat of another long walk through the lovely ancient city. As the daylight faded the colours of all the flowers seemed to burn against the softened shades of stone and brick with an air of contrivance, as if deliberately set for a theatrical show. The streets were quiet at this hour, the rush of traffic over and the evening's pleasure round not yet begun. A friendly basset hound accompanied me for a good distance, then suddenly, as if he had come to the limit of his territory, wheeled about and with a courteous wag of his tail made off.

In Watergate Street I came upon a pub which lured me into its lounge (that curious word which seems to have replaced

18

the old saloon and probably comes from America) by a notice on the door. This said that persons in working clothes or of untidy appearance could not be served in there but must go to the public bar. It sounded a reassuring note, suggestive of order and *tenue* worthy of our patrician surroundings; but the room itself was full of frowsy mophaired teenagers smoking like chimneys and with a juke box blaring its head off. Wondering what their working clothes could be like, if they had any or indeed ever worked at all, I took a hasty departure.

I had better luck in Northgate Street, where another attractive old inn was juke box-free and where entertainment was provided as rich in its way as that of the Pied Bull. It came from one of the most lethal bores I ever encountered, haranguing a captive audience of the two unfortunate women behind the bar, on and on, about his thoughts, deeds and experience over the years. It was very much like *The Diary of a Nobody*, related not by a couple of lively wits but by a Pooter himself, a Pooter gifted with total recall, able to fill out the smallest event with a wealth of insignificant detail, pausing only from time to time to take a pull at his beer.

I took advantage of one such break to give my order and then sat down a little way off to enjoy the performance. One of the women brought my drink across and broke so far with public-house etiquette as to growl at me, a stranger: 'That man will be the death of us.'

'Yes', the fellow was blithely proceeding, 'I love a boiled onion. But it don't love me. Not now, it don't. Time was, I could eat any amount of 'em at a go. One Christmas I ate a coupla dozen. But now, if I only take one, it seems to round on me, like. Funny thing, that. There's nothing wrong with me either, the medico says. Just can't manage a boiled onion.'

Presently his eye fell on the clock. 'Oh my, I've missed the Wrexham bus. It'll be leaving this minute. And there isn't another, not for an hour.'

Galvanized, the women eagerly pointed out that the bus would stop on its way not fifty yards from their door and if he looked sharp he could catch it. He hesitated, then reluctantly took his hat from the peg and turned towards the door. Now the women's faces were lit with happy smiles.

19

But he turned again, hung up his hat and waved his empty mug at them.

'No, I'll trouble you for a refill,' he said, confident of his welcome. 'Me sprinting days are over.'

Their faces suddenly long again, they drew the beer and resigned themselves to another hour of torment. The things some people have to do for a living hardly bear contemplation. I wondered if this were a daily mortification and whether the lack of other custom here were in any way linked to it. It has been said that Hitler, before he came to power, could empty a Bierkeller in roughly twenty minutes: one would have liked to see the pair in competition.

By now darkness had fallen, the street lamps were out and what with the graceful towers and arches, the harmony of all visible things and the masses of bloom, Chester was what travel writers are wont to describe as 'a veritable fairyland'. But just as in Eden itself a serpent reared his head, here too was a blot on the near-perfection. The noise pouring out from discos and juke boxes at every few yards, 'music' of a kind one would have thought that only a savage could bear, let alone enjoy, seemed like a long howl of defiance. It was as if those young barbarians revelling in it were shouting at their civilized forebears, 'So much for you!' Goodness knows, I have been in noisy places enough, the Orient, Spain, the West Indies and so on, but there one expects it. Formerly a love of peace and quiet was characteristic of the English at every social level. You read of labourers, for example, giving as excuse for battering a baby that nothing else would stop its screaming. But the most vociferous baby on earth could never hold its own with what the rising generation now listens to of choice, and with intense satisfaction. If the Spanish author Azorínas was right in thinking that 'the degree of sensitivity – and hence of civilisation – of any people can partly be measured by the extent to which they will tolerate noise,' it would seem that we are heading for the jungle.

And when, after dinner, I reached my hotel, the disco there was again in full cry. This was a blow, for the now friendly and solicitous staff had told me it only broke out at the weekend. Either they had formed the habit, also new in England, of saying whatever would please the hearer or the weekend itself had changed, taking in Monday, which was today, and for all I knew, Tuesday as well.

What was to be done? I could bear no more of it. The official guide had a list of hotels, hostels and clubs and I began looking them over, trying to guess from their names where peace might be found. There were some charming names among them, Abbot's Well, Blossoms, Coach and Horses, the Golden Lion, Plantation, Saddle – but what guarantee was there in these dark days that the establishment would live up to them?

Right at the end, last of all, was one which could not be other than it seemed. It was The Retreat House, in Abbey Square, and it had a Warden. A voice, kind and firm and which somehow went with the address, answered the telephone. Yes, it said, there was a vacant room, but did I realize what kind of house this was? Evidently, there were restrictions on entry. Somewhat uneasily, I admitted to being a Catholic. 'Oh, *that* doesn't matter,' the voice said briskly, 'the question is, what are you looking for?' Anywhere that didn't have a disco. Very well, then. And you will come tomorrow? What time?

The house was deliciously quiet and spotlessly clean, managed by Anglican nuns, with little notices here and there requesting the inmates to do this or not to do that which brought up memories of boarding-school. It was next door to the Bishop's residence and a few doors away from that of the Canon. The other guests at my table were a clergyman's wife and daughter, who told funny stories about the bishops they knew, a Scottish divine who had political differences with his bellringer, which he described to us but kept from that functionary lest the service be withdrawn, and a young parson *de nos jours*, tweedy, leftwing and with an accent and grammar that the BBC would call Usage. We cleared away after meals, made our own beds and conducted ourselves with decorum. My room on the second floor looked over the Square itself, with the flowering shrubs, the clergy walking about on their calm orderly business and few sounds of any kind apart from the Cathedral bells.

It was all the better for the suffering that had gone before. The old chestnut about the lunatic who banged himself on the head with a hammer because it was so agreeable when he left off, took on a new meaning. Perhaps what England needs today is a radical transformation, an end to the notion that people are all alike, a splitting up into categories, *apartheid* in fact. Noise-lovers might be segregated in special haunts and forbidden to wander afield. One of the benefits conferred on the country by Billy Butlin was precisely that: he drew them off, as a poultice draws a boil, and subjected them to an iron control; and what private enterprise achieved on a modest scale could serve as a model for similar improvement on a national.

A few days later the Canon sent me an invitation to sherry. As I was not expecting correspondence, I came on it quite by chance among the letters, pamphlets, silver crosses and other *objets divers* for sale on the hall table a very few minutes before the time he mentioned. He opened the door himself, as he had done on my previous visit: there seemed to be no staff in the house, although what I saw of it was immaculate.

He gave me a glass of excellent *fino* and we settled down. I raised the subject of madmen in Cathedrals and what brought them there, for the fascination such places seem to have for a troubled mind has always interested me. Kilvert has a paragraph on this, informed by Sir Gilbert Lewis, a Canon of Worcester, who told him that mad people were apt to come there. There was a woman who gave a great deal of trouble by screeching out and a Mr Quarrell who used to make antics at the time of the Communion. His movements were so extraordinary that all had to watch them and the authorities were at a loss to know what to do as he did nothing to warrant exclusion. 'Ah,' said Sir Gilbert, 'you don't know all the little games that go on in cathedrals!'

I had seen an odd performance myself as I left after Evensong the day before. A man with a battered old hat firmly on his head was leaning against a pillar and shouting at the

22

top of his lungs, exactly what I could not hear. The Canon put a few questions as to his general appearance, height, clothing and so on, and was easily able to identify him. 'One of our regulars – we have several, all quite harmless.' He spoke with kindly, even affectionate, tolerance but had no views on what may have brought them there. It did seem strange. When we get the occasional nut in, say, Westminster Cathedral, it is usually a Protestant Truth Society one, bent on denouncing the Scarlet Woman; and such a one is dealt with swiftly and silently by some of the smoothest chuckers-out in London. But those who hang about an Anglican place apparently have no message to give, seldom interrupt a service or give any real trouble at all.

Our conversation was briefly interrupted by the Bishop tearing in, giving a message, saying a few kind words to me and tearing out again. The Anglican want of starch is highly agreeable and so is the ease with which the clergy and laymen can talk together, and even argue. With our own clerics, however genial they may be, there is always a certain restraint, one is always, so to speak, on the receiving end. I remember an Irish Monsignor with whom I was on very friendly terms once making a generalization about the Italian people which struck me as so absurd that before I could stop myself I exclaimed, 'No, no, you're quite wrong there.' The sudden flash of wrath in those blue eyes, I remember still. On another occasion that stormy petrel and brilliant writer told a parish priest and dear friend of his that he was a bloody fool. There was an ominous hush: I fairly shook in my shoes. After a while, the father said slowly, 'No one has called me that since I was ordained.' There was another pause while he pondered this epoch-making event, and then he added pensively, 'Maybe it does every one good, to be called a bloody fool from time to time.'

Let me hasten to add that I had no wish or reason to call my present host a bloody fool or any other disobliging thing: he was a most interesting and stimulating companion, but to sit and freely exchange ideas with a man of the cloth was a new experience. I was to see him once again, when I called to say goodbye with a pot of home-made marmalade from a Coffee Morning at the Retreat House, and was promptly drawn in for more sherry and conversation. The pleasures of my stay in that beautiful city were much enhanced by this personal contact; and from a foolish diffidence I had nearly passed it by.

Chapter Four

I headed now for Worcester, a city I had briefly visited in the past and longed to explore. The best way of getting there seemed to be by coach from Wrexham, a roundabout journey but good for seeing the countryside and towns it went through. There was only one a day, and therefore a taxi was ordered in plenty of time, leaving a margin for accidents. One of the Retreat House nuns found me pacing fretfully up and down fifteen minutes after it should have been there and revealed, too late, that the firm was anything but reliable. A telephone call drew an assurance that the car was on its way, and so did a second, more urgent, one twelve minutes later, although one could have walked from the garage in half that time. At last it appeared, driven by a surly youth in oily jeans, who replied to my recriminations with 'Don't blame me, luv, not my business'.

He apparently took a narrow view of his business altogether, for he made no move to help with the luggage, open the cab door or provide any other such frill; and when we got to Wrexham he casually inquired if I knew where the coach stop was. Of course I did not, having never been to Wrexham before, and I suggested with no little warmth that he might have found it out before he started. This too he said was none of his business, which was merely to drive. I bade him ask: he did so and was cheerfully misdirected a couple of times. Evidently the Welsh share the Irish reluctance to admit their ignorance, preferring to send the hapless questioner miles out of his way. The town was large, sprawling and mainly hideous with a whole area of plain square buildings like roadblocks, as if all effort to build even the semblance of a house had been abandoned. Round and round we went until in despair I bawled out to a traffic policeman and we finally were put on the right road.

25

Luckily the coach was late in setting off, as it should have been gone a good quarter hour by now. Several rows of seats to the fore were marked *No Smoking* and a place at the very front was free. I took it gladly, thinking how much better things were in this respect than they used to be – only to find that the driver considered himself a special case and puffed away at a chain of gaspers for the two and three-quarter hours of the trip.

A crony and one-time colleague sat immediately behind him and they compared old times with the present, to the detriment of the former.

'You only had to be a coupla minutes late and they'd stand you off,' the driver observed, in warm approval of the march of progress.

'Ah. Bloody clock-watchers.'

'And uniform? don't talk to me. Why, you dussent take so much as your cap off, even in the country.'

'Inspectors all over the shop.'

'The passengers were as bad and worse. Complaining of this and that. And you had to take notice on 'em. Now you just say nothin', or tell 'em no one else has objected. They soon pack it in.'

By now we had reached the outskirts of the town and the driver pulled up in order to divest himself of tunic and cap and light another gasper. Then the coach went on and the conversation was resumed, beneath a notice forbidding anyone to speak to the driver or distract him in any way.

It was a beautiful ride in this beautiful time of the year, with primroses covering every bank, herds of cattle with satiny black and white coats, their calves lying peacefully in the sun and pigs with large floppy ears, of the distinctive Saddleback breed with fore- and hindquarters of inky blue and a wide pink cummerbund in the middle. Pheasants broke from cover with a cry like a faulty klaxon and scuttled away across the ploughed land in the belief that our coach was after them. The whole scene was delightfully varied. We passed through little towns or villages with charming old-world shops, timbered houses built long ago and leaning to one side or apparently about to collapse altogether, crooked lanes turning off a main street, and everywhere the warm yellow forsythia and the rosy magnolia buds. The signboards of the public houses were unusually good as if they had been carefully painted by someone who put his heart into it. There would be a squirrel, thoughtfully examining a nut between his paws, a bull that looked like a bull and not an advertisement for Oxo, a golden lion that might have leapt from a mediaeval tapestry. These little places had a wonderfully relaxed and peaceful air about them, too. The people walked along so leisurely, they hardly seemed to be going anywhere in particular and one never passed another without stopping to chat. The dogs took their time as well, and I thought the very ducks were waddling more slowly than ducks are wont to do.

One by one we left them behind and were out in the country again, through rolling meadows with their tidy hedges and small dark woods like so many islands, or up a steep hill under a ceiling of branches in new leaf or past a lake with various kinds of waterfowl all courting like mad. Blonde little girls trotted by on smart little ponies, serious and businesslike in their jockey caps and skintight jodhpurs. Now and then a hare might be seen, capering about a field in a manic springtime dance. In the distance were the slender graceful spires of churches, backed by a line of low blue hills. The rooks were building high this year, noisy and self-important as ever, and screeching at the squirrels who came frisking up to watch them. I was glad that I had no car and could take things in while somebody else did the driving.

The journey passed without incident except when we paused at Shrewsbury, to let some people off and take some others up. Then a young man asked the driver to hold on while he went for a cup of tea; and it was edifying to hear that official explain that much as he would have liked to oblige him, rules were rules and unauthorized delays forbidden: and further, that if you did it for one you had to do it for all, with the probable diaspora of the whole crowd before you knew where you were.

At Worcester our national gift for mismanagement was revealed in the full force of its ingenuity. It might have been expected that the coach would make for the terminal, with its cloak and waiting rooms, its left luggage office and taxi rank;

and apart from these amenities the other cross-country buses started from there, which would have eased matters somewhat for those on board who had to make a connection. But not a bit of it. On we sailed to a private halting-place of its own, away from everywhere, outside a dismal sandwich bar, no telephone, no taxi, no left luggage, all seemingly arranged with an eye to the traveller's maximum discomfort.

I asked the man in the sandwich bar if he would mind my heavy suitcase while I went in search of a cab. His face was immediately transformed by a beaming smile. 'Not a hope!' he replied. 'We don't take no responsibilities,' put in a female colleague, beaming likewise. Less deadly than the male, however, she informed me that the guard in a car park across the road would sometimes keep an eye on luggage, to 'oblige'. But the guard, on being appealed to, said that he was shortly going off and, this being Friday, his Relief might turn up and then again he might not. There was never no telling what that bloke might do.

Ah, for the commercially minded Continent where, for an appropriate sum, people will do almost anything! Picking up my bag, I trudged away towards the spires of Worcester, standing out against the horizon. At the coach terminal, puffing and blowing like a horse who has just won the Derby, I made for the left luggage. Here there was a longish wait, as the custodian was deep in discussion about the weekend soccer fixtures; but at last our business was settled and, in urgent need of restoratives, I took a cab to the centre of the town.

The Cathedral clock was just striking two when the cab drew up, and on going into the first tavern I saw, I found that Worcester had the caprice of shutting at this hour instead of half-past. The lady behind the bar was trying to convince a German that this was so. He was a Teuton of the old school to look at, with cropped hair, a square head and a roll of fat at the nape of his neck. Glaring round him, he asked belligerently why, in that case, all present were drinking. They were not, she explained: they were Drinking Up. The foreign visitor expressed a wish to join them in whatever they might be doing. The lady explained that he could not Drink Up unless he had something to do it with. But he could have a slice of *pizza*, she added kindly.

'You shall sell me a bottle, so, and I shall bear her away,' the German howled.

'That's against the law, dear,' she added, quick as a flash and with that peculiar glee I had noted in the sandwich bar couple. 'But why not have a nice bit of *pizza*?' she persisted. 'On'y made this morning.'

The German angrily shook his head and swept out. All over his large red face was the iron resolve to travel elsewhere in the future. And then something occurred which revealed all too clearly the state of law and order in our decadent land. With a wink the bar lady asked what I would have and cheerfully served it, requesting me to Drink Up like a luv, lest she go to quod. She reckoned I was all right, she said, whereas that foreign chap could be anyone, not foreign at all perhaps but a peeler in disguise. You needed your wits about you, in her trade.

The man had simply got her back up, of course, in the effortless German way, but you could see his point. To anyone from the Continent the licensing laws of England must seem the height of perversity. For that matter they did so to me after my very few days at Chester. I knew all about the permitted hours, which were reasonable enough, but there were a host of petty restrictions within that framework that seemed to make no sense whatever. Why should persons under eighteen be refused liquor inside a pub when friends can bring them whatever they want outside the door, until they fall flat on their faces if so inclined? And why, after Time! is called, are ten minutes allowed for drinking up what you have but not for buying more to take away? Even mild amusements in the permitted hours are regulated by the Betting and Gaming Act of 1960. With the consent of the licensee, for example, the following may be played for small stakes in the public rooms: darts, billiards, dominoes, skittles, cribbage and shove ha'penny. But what precisely is meant by a small stake? A trifle to you may be a serious matter to me. And the playing of any game not listed above is illegal. It might be wise to ban roulette or poker, but suppose you had a sudden powerful urge to chance your arm at

Scrabble, beggar-my-neighbour or Snakes and Ladders? Would you land yourself in the dock? And who puts all this nonsense together and gets Parliament, that glorious institution and guardian of our liberty, to clap it on to the Statute Book? Some kind of para-schoolteacher, it may be, forever forbidding this and enjoining that. Perhaps of recent years he has rather overplayed his hand, losing the support of even the docile English. At all events, there I peacefully sat, the forbidden wine in my fist and a toasted sandwich on the way.

Afterwards I went to the Tourist Office in the Guildhall to get a list of places to stay at. The Guildhall is an ornate building by a pupil of Wren and at present was being spring-cleaned and the figures on the façade, Queen Anne above the main entrance, Charles I and Charles II on either side, were fresh in their red gold and blue. Among other decorations is a severed head, nailed by the ears, supposed to be that of Cromwell. Worcester Civitas in Bello et Pace Fidelis, prides itself on its long royalist tradition and particularly its support of the Crown during the Civil War. In the booklet the Tourist Office gave me, Mr Peter Walker, the local Member of Parliament, declared that it did everything in its power to defend King Charles II when he arrived there with his Scottish army in 1651. The facts are rather different, however. The King called up every man between 16 and 60 but, despite their motto, they were in no great hurry to stir. The Royal army had a mere 16,000 men, mostly Scots, against Cromwell's 28,000, and the old bogey won the battle for all the nailed ears on his effigy.

Knowing no more of Worcester than I had of Chester, I decided to choose my lodging by divination as I always do in strange places abroad. My powers in this direction are somewhat erratic, and the results can be appalling, but this time I was lucky. The house stood on the bank of the river Severn, in a garden that was cared for but not fussed over, with a fringe of trees and bushes that threw a green reflection of themselves upside down into the water. All along the bank on the other side sat a row of impassive fishermen, hour after hour, who as far as I could see never caught anything at all. Bouncy big dogs, chows, labradors, retrievers, raced up and down the towpath under the hotel garden wall and barked merrily at every boat that passed by.

It was a homely ramshackle place, mainly used by sportsmen of one kind and another, and run with agreeable nonchalance. While registering, I noticed a box of letters stamped ready for posting which were still there a day or so later. Clearly, time was not of the essence. But deliveries to the hotel were likewise made in a spirit of relaxation. From a window next morning I observed a man pushing what looked like a baby's pram slowly up the drive, rather as tinkers push their wares from door to door. Nothing in his apparel or demeanour suggested it, but he turned out to be Her Majesty's postman. Having fished a bundle of correspondence out of the pram he handed it to the hotel receptionist, who had hastened out to meet him, no doubt for fear that he might over-exert himself; and he paused for a chat before continuing his round at the same measured pace as before.

On the river side of the house was a kind of platform under an awning, where you could sit and drink and watch the boats, as pleasant as watching the Paris crowds from a cafe. There were canoes and sculling boats manned by boys from the King's School nearby, a few smart motor launches and barges galore, hired out to holiday makers, mostly young and without previous experience of navigation.

I spoke to one, a girl from Birmingham, who was exploring the river with three friends. Up to last year she had never been off dry land in her life, but now she was quite at ease in boats and crazy about them. Their management, fuelling, steering, tying up, presented no problem, the one difficulty being the negotiation of locks. In a homely Brum accent she told me of the various adventures and mishaps that had befallen them, all taken in their stride with great good humour. I found their pluck and enterprise very admirable, and also their taste in preferring a holiday like this to a routine package abroad.

Altogether it was a charming place and I enjoyed it immensely. All the arrangements were sensible and humane, and there was no regimentation of any kind. If you wanted to eat out, you could, if not, no one confronted you with a grisly

31

fixed meal. You could have an excellent dinner à la carte, entertained by lively Italian waiters, or otherwise you could have a snack from the buffet. If you were tired, you could have breakfast in bed and lie there afterwards, with no one hunting you out on the pretext of having to make your bed. Telephone messages were accurately taken and delivered, if not always at once, and there were two friendly mischievous dogs to give a touch of home. And it was not at all dear. My powers of divination do often let me down, as I have said, but when they work they are apt to do it in style.

Chapter Five

The well-produced and lavishly illustrated Guide to Worcester is something of a curiosity. You would expect a publication of that sort to pick out all that was most attractive, photograph it to the best advantage and discreetly ignore whatever was ugly. But it appears to glory in Worcester's shame. Either in a spirit of candour or because no one realizes how dreadful they are, quite a number of eyesores have been included. The Technical College, a box, is proudly displayed, but right-thinking people could not possibly wish to see it; and the same applies to the Girls' Grammar School, another box, the City Youth Centre, which defies description, the grandstand of the racecourse, a replica of others all over the world, and a view of Cripplegate Park, with trees and a herbaceous border in front of three High Rises.

That is not to say the beauties are altogether neglected. There are shots of the Cathedral, the river, the parks and ancient monuments, the old Commandery for instance, which was not a barracks but a religious hospital whose Priors took a notion to style themselves Commanders, the house where Charles II hid after his great defeat and, of course, that resplendent Guildhall. But so many more were there for the finding, odd corners of little old lanes, lovely quiet squares with delicious gardens, the view of the whole city from the high road that runs along one side with the Malvern hills in the background, delightful boating scenes in the Diglis Basin where the Birmingham canal meets the Severn. There is endless pleasure in simply wandering about and coming on these treasures, a feast for the eye and imagination, whereas the gruesome products of our age may surely be taken for granted.

On the whole, a rather Philistine spirit seems to prevail among those in charge of publicity. I was startled to read in a leaflet or mini guide that Worcester 'is specially known for its porcelain, gloves and sauce', with the added appeal of the *Berrow's Journal* and the cricketing ground. Frankly, none of these, admirable enough in their way, spring first to my own mind in connection with it, but rather the romance of its past, the glorious music still to be heard in its Cathedral, the noble Cathedral itself and the delectable nooks and crannies abounding everywhere.

A fascinating little building, though far from beautiful, is Lady Huntingdon's chapel in Deansway. It is not thought worthy of mention in the Guide but is merely lumped in with miscellaneous places of worship, together with Latterday Saints, Elim Pentecostal, Zion and other exotics. I came across it when briefly in Worcester some years ago and straightway took a liking for it. Squat and roundish in form, it was something like an igloo but built in warm old brick, and the interior was bare as it could possibly be: a plain altar with the Commandments written large on either side, a roomy pulpit and high comfortless wooden pews were its only furnishing. It had great atmosphere nevertheless, and fairly reeked of nonconformist piety, although the Countess who set it up belonged to the Church of England. She was much influenced by the Methodist George Whitefield, who seems to have provided a butt for certain wags of the day: he is the Squintum portrayed in Samuel Foote's comedy *The Minor* and has ridicule heaped on him by Richard Graves in *The Spiritual Quixote*, a merry novel published in 1772. But he was much admired by the noble and serious lady, who appointed him her domestic chaplain and fervently supported the Methodist connection he started, allowing him to call it by her name. This odd deviation was caused, as so often happens, by hostility to something else, as she had an implacable loathing for the bishops of the church that was properly hers.

I had to pass it on my way to the Public Library and looked forward to finding it peacefully dotty as ever; but to my grief it was locked, derelict in appearance with broken dirty windows and drifts of paper lying about the courtyard. Perhaps after standing firm a couple of centuries or so it had been too badly shaken by the lorries of today. Next door there was a firm of builders and decorators, and I went in to make enquiries. Apparently the Corporation had declared it unsafe and asked the Trustees to put it in order. This they would not do, so that it 'fell into the Corporation's lap again', my informant said, broadly smiling – it is notable, by the way, that references to Worcester Corporation are wont to be accompanied either by mirth or an explosion of fury – and would have to be preserved if at all as a national monument.

This would have been an appropriate and respectable end; but, as appeared later, it was not to be. One day the evening paper came out with a screaming headline, 'City Offered £5 for Chapel!' The Worcester Preservation Trust wanted it bought from the owners and made over to them for this nominal sum, whereupon they would go to work collecting funds for transforming it into a music centre. The amounts mentioned were enough to make one giddy, the estimated cost of repair being about £175,000 with another £75,000 for conversion. These were fine round sums for a small round building which had modestly stood there so long and where I had never encountered a living soul. I had some doubts as to the Founder's approval of the project: indeed, a vision by no means disagreeable came into my mind, of her Ladyship manifesting herself at the inauguration and bidding the assembly begone.

All that lay in the future, of course, and may have been a pipedream anyhow. Perhaps the site will be cleared to make room for a garage. On this sunny afternoon I merely stood awhile and mourned the little place I used to enjoy.

I was making for the Public Library in order to read the daily newspaper there. It had been my intention to get a copy in Wrexham but the demon cabby put paid to that and in Worcester every last one had gone. The stuffy true-blue journal I like, so derided by thinkers and seers, invariably sells out before the rest, and with the election coming on I was loth to miss a single issue.

But when I got to the Library its copy was in use, not by one of the suburban housewives or retired military men who are popularly believed to make up its readership but by a mechanic in overalls. In the hall outside the reading room were two displays of an entertaining and instructive nature

35

to pass the time while I waited. One consisted of empty beer bottles, amazing in the variety of shape and size, with a note to say that more could be seen in the Museum upstairs. The other was a collection of Teddy Bears, dating from about 1910 to the present time, lent by a public-spirited local resident, with a short history of that engaging animal. It seemed that in 1903 a cartoonist, Clifford Merryman, did a sketch of Theodore Roosevelt refusing to shoot a cub and called it Teddy's Bear, whereupon a smart fellow in the soft toy line snapped it up and launched it on the market; and very soon Teddy Bears were sweeping first America, then England and Europe, and finally the world. How successfully and completely I can vouch for, as once in far-off Tokyo at Christmas time a mammoth store on the Ginza had given pride of place at the top of the tree not to a fairy or Father Christmas but to a cute little crucified Teddy Bear. But it was in England that they cast their greatest spell, putting dolls and bunnies in the shade and even vying with the much loved Golly, now swept away by race relations fanatics.

Nor was their following confined to the nursery. A whole middle-class generation fed their minds on the simple thoughts of Winnie the Pooh, the aristocratic hero of *Brideshead Revisited* was never without his own dear cuddlesome boy, and our Poet Laureate fully shares that devotion. One of those active American anthropologists might do worse than give the matter attention, as it is quite as interesting and much more mysterious than the fetishes of Africa.

And here a rich assortment of them sat, dark brown or blond, stout or rangy, their faces expressive of no great intellectual power but benign and reassuring. I must have lingered over them for on going back to the reading room I found the mechanic had gone and his place taken by what looked to be a tramp, with long white hair to his shoulders and broken boots. The newcomer had a mind of his own, however, for he was hard at work annotating the leader page of the paper, probably with an *I agree* here and *I disagree* there, as thoughtful library users so often will. Or perhaps he was merely correcting the misprints, with what practical aim it was hard to imagine, but with work enough to detain him until the library should close. In either case, the outlook was unpromising. Some people will have a virgin paper or none: I am not quite so fussy but I draw the line at one enriched by comments, however apt or profound. And so I called it a day and went to walk by the river instead.

That evening I asked at the hotel if there were steamer trips on the river, this being a delicious way of enjoying country, and was advised to seek out a man called Brian.

'You should find him down at the harbour,' they said, 'although he moves about a good deal.'

Next morning I set off along the towpath on this errand, accompanied by a friendly and inquisitive Chow. We passed the Training Ship Fearless, which was not a ship but a school for sea cadets, and eventually came to a real little harbour at the path's end, with locks and bridges and boat-building sheds. A new vessel, built for a man in the South of France, was being launched from one of their yards, with a crowd of old salts looking on and freely offering advice. The whole atmosphere was nautical, and refreshing in landlocked Worcester.

Brian, they told me here, might well be in the Anchor Inn. This was a place of character and full of more old watermen, in which I learned that he would most likely be found in the Alma up the road. There, a pretty girl agreed that Brian – whose name she uttered with reverence – did often look in, but he was a man of wide business interests and might be anywhere. His office was beneath my own hotel, and I would know if he was in it when his Jag was parked outside. In fact a glossy green Jaguar had caught my eye in the hotel grounds as I was setting forth to look for him. The hotel had mentioned no such circumstance but it did not matter, a wild-goose chase can be very good fun. The Alma, like the Anchor, had much to commend it in the way of company, and there was a fascinating set of rules hanging on the wall:

> Fourpence a night for a bed
> Sixpence, with pot luck
> Twopence for horsekeeping
> No more than 5 to sleep in one bed
> No razor grinders or tinkers taken in

No dogs allowed in the kitchen
Organgrinders to sleep in the kitchen.
Lemuel Cox's Inn.

Unhappily, there is no date to this document.

The green Jaguar was still parked in the hotel grounds, at the top of a few steps leading down to the door of Brian's cave-like office. This proved to be about the size of a yacht's cabin, strewn with files and papers, and hardly went with the Jaguar. Brian was a big handsome amiable man, sharply dressed, with a heavy gold bangle on one arm and bulky gold rings on most of his fingers, and there was an air of controlled power about him, such as we see in the chuckers-out of night-clubs. Hearing that I wanted to join one of his trips, he consulted a ledger and said that the first open night was not for three weeks, the boat leaving at eight.

I said that sounded a bit early, because the hotel staff drowsed of a morning and I did not want to start off without any breakfast.

'Early?' he repeated. 'Eight o'clock at night?'

It turned out that his boats were not for the tranquil viewing of spires, woodlands, hills and pastoral scenes but provided a floating disco for the din-crazy youth of the town. In fact, I had witnessed the departure of one such craft the night before, with garish lights looped round the deck and making a horrible row, and had heard it coming back as well in the wee hours of the morning. And so another dream was ended. Brian fully understood that it was not my line and regretted the disappointment.

As I went away, two clients of a more appropriate description rode up on Honda motor-bikes that roared like angry lions. Both had carrotty hair streaming over their shoulders, with close-fitting metal caps on their heads, such as Hengist and Horsa might have worn, and black leather tunics with skulls and crossbones and other daunting insignia stuck all over them. This get-up may have related to some vision, or ideal, of themselves which boosted their morale, but did not seem to go with the friendly boyish grins they gave me or the marked respect they showed to the maestro. And indeed he gave the impression of being a match for any number of them.

I went along the river bank and through a gloomy tunnel up some stairs into the sunny Cathedral Close. There was a lunatic on a bicycle pedalling wildly round and round the lawn, with a transistor as mad as himself going full tilt, while parsonical beings watched him benignly through their windows. Evidently, he was a recurring phenomenon and Worcester drew such people to itself, as noted by the Reverend Francis Kilvert. Kilvert once spent a while in this same close, in a house that is standing yet, although opinions differ as to which it is. I thought of him again this morning because of a passage in the Diary relating to tourists, already, it would seem, a pest in 1870: 'What was our horror on entering the enclosure to see two tourists with staves and shoulder belts all complete postured among the ruins in an attitude of admiration, one of them discoursing learnedly to his companion and pointing out objects of interest with his stick. If there is one thing more hateful than another, it is being told what to admire and having objects pointed out to one with a stick. Of all noxious animals too the most noxious is a tourist. And of all tourists the most vulgar, illbred, offensive and loathsome is the British tourist.'

For the tourists were out in strength, and if the mere pointing of a stick had so enraged him, what he could have seen here today might have carried him off altogether. For instance, there was an enormously fat blowsy woman, middle-aged, bare-legged, in a flowered print dress well above her bun-like knees, fondling a stray cat conscripted for the purpose while a friend, or was it her twin, took a snap; and as if that were not gruesome enough, she was posed against the Cathedral, with a moronic smile on her face that had to be seen to be believed. Kilvert little knew what a sheltered life he led, in those happy far-off days of Queen Victoria. I watched, spellbound, as the photograph was taken, the camera changed hands, likewise the cat, and the whole affecting scene was enacted again, with two memorable pictures for their albums no doubt of 'Myself with Pussy, Worcester Cathedral in Background'.

Or, if the Reverend Kilvert managed to survive this, within the Cathedral there was what might have given him the coup de grâce. Excellent Christian though he was, his views could hardly be described as liberal or ecumenical. 'Some barbarian – a dissenter no doubt, probably a Baptist,' he wrote grimly on one occasion, 'has cut down the silver birches on the Little Mountain near Cefw y Fedwas . . . '

Pleasanter thoughts supervened as I walked through the Cloister and heard the voices of the choir lifted in practice. The Worcester choir can hold its own with any in England, and its members are chosen and trained with great care. They have to pass a general test for the King's Grammar School before being given an audition; the requirements then are an ability to sing in tune, a good musical memory, good pitch and good tone; and here, as on the Continent, the natural, rather hard tone is favoured above the soft and sweet. They must be between 8 and 9½ years of age, and must leave the choir at 14, whether their voices have broken or not; and they must play one instrument already, and take up a second when they begin with the choir. In making his choice among the candidates, Dr Hunt the choirmaster and organist looks out for the smaller boys, other things being equal, as the voices of the large tend to break sooner. There were twenty of them in the choir at this moment, plus three little creatures who sit with them in plain clothes and behave with the utmost circumspection: these were the probationers, or 'babies' as they are called. The boys used to come from all over the country, Wales, Devon, the North, but now they seem to be mainly local. With the consent of the Dean and the school, they do a lot of outside work, recitals and recordings, and many of them go on to a musical career when they leave school. One chorister became organist to Westminster Cathedral, another at St Albans, and another Organ Scholar at King's, Cambridge; and there was a youth in the present choir whom I had seen directing operations at Evensong the day before, and who looked like a born conductor.

One thing about the choir did puzzle me rather, listening to them now, and that was their speech. I had already passed little groups from their school conversing to a man in the dire accents commonly heard these days; and yet these particular boys were singing in pure good English. I subsequently asked Dr Hunt about this, and he thought the singing they had to do in foreign languages, Italian, German and so on, might have a beneficial effect, at any rate, on their vowels. If that is so, the sooner every child in England is put through the same hoop the better; but then, why not speak well all the time? Perhaps the 'posh' or 'snob' way of pronouncing – I have heard both these terms used by professional linguisticians – may seem to the choir like a foreign tongue in itself, into which they slip as they put their surplices on and discard as they take them off.

I stood and listened with the greatest pleasure awhile, as they repeated their phrases over and over like so many thrushes until they were perfect.

Then I went out into the streets again. These were in such contrast to the peace and order of the Cathedral that it was like entering a different world. It was the week-end and the town wore a new aspect: everywhere was filth, with plastic bags, empty bottles, ice-cream cartons, strewn about as the young made merry in their own peculiar way. Two ape-like creatures, one male, one female, were selling a newssheet with the huge headline WANTED FOR MURDER!, the wanted man being a police officer who allegedly had killed the agitator Blair Peach at Southall with a blow of his truncheon. They were flourishing the rag in people's faces and shouting at them if they did not take it. Gangs of others roamed the pavements or squatted on them, dirty, greasy, dishevelled, some with their hair dyed improbable purples, oranges and greens, nearly all in black leather jerkins, likewise shouting at the passersby or playing their folk-music on mouth organs or guitars. Evidently, they wanted to be alarming, but were more pathetic than anything else, with the gaiety that belongs to youth entirely absent.

One little group I came on made a deep impression on me. A very young policeman with blond hair and apple cheeks was facing half a dozen or so of the toughies and lashing them with his tongue. 'Now then, come on out with it,' he was saying. 'Some of you must have seen something, and if you won't tell me and I have to find it out for myself, there's going to be bloody 'ell!' In just that way I have seen young soldiers in Belfast stand up to a teenage mob, calm and self-assured, while the others, about the same age, from a similar background more or less, muttered and snarled but dared do

41

nothing. What produces the extraordinary difference between them, perhaps the sociologists can explain.

I dropped into a pub in the High Street and found its small front parlour occupied by four girls, all shrieking with laughter, on and on, apparently about nothing. Every so often their breath gave out and they stopped, panting, for a few moments until one struck up again and they all joined in. Not a single word was spoken by any, what the joke could possibly be was a mystery, and they just screamed merrily on until, on a sudden impulse, they rose and ran out of the snug in a body.

The landlord was busy in the larger bar behind, attending to yet more youngsters, who appeared to be of a comparatively serious disposition. They were gravely taking the world to pieces and setting it right, shaking their heads over the government and the downward trend of the nation. It was all most edifying, but presently the landlord came through to me, laughing, and supplied some details. Not one of these thinkers had worked in his or her life, and they were in and out of the courts 'like yo-yos'. The night before, being Friday when they collected their dole, they had drunk wine and brandy mixed together and later had fallen off the lock into the river. None could swim, one had nearly drowned and was given the kiss of life. Others had been up before the beak for squatting in an empty school and using the gas and electricity which had not been cut off: that was apparently all they could be charged with, although they had left the whole building in a horrible mess. Only a few of them came in here, the landlord said, because he gave no credit and stood no nonsense, but if I was interested in Worcester as it really was and not merely in what the tourist office put out, I had better go round to The Plough in Fish Street. That was their headquarters, where they drank every day on tic, squaring up when they got their weekly dole.

I found this interesting centre easily enough, a few doors away from the highly respectable and bourgeois Farrier's Arms, and it was just as the landlord had described it, jampacked with the T-shirted brigade, most of them with an air of belonging and all giving out a poignant badger-like smell. There were two bars, each hardly bigger than a roomy horse-box, in one of which darts were flying about and narrowly missing the serried heads below and in the other a juke box was howling reggae at a pitch that would have amply filled a football stadium. Here, nevertheless, the lads were in deep and earnest talk, speaking in normal tones and hearing each other plainly, as it seems factory workers can do amid the racket of great machines. The proprietor was very civil, even to addressing me with the archaic Madam, while the customers behaved as if I were not there at all, a characteristic of their kind *en masse* although separately they will often engage in conversation, and very amusingly too: now, the nearest thing to a sign of welcome was the great broad grin of naked flesh whenever they leaned forward. I had a drink and left, stunned by a mere five minutes in what to them was a cosy and congenial little home from home.

The city did indeed appear to be overrun and occupied by an army of teenaged Goths. Nevertheless, I found a refuge in an inn just by the main bus station where I wanted to make some enquiries. I had noticed it the day before, and now asked the meaning of its attractive name. One man confidently said that it was an ancient hall of justice, but another overheard him and butted in to say that, on the contrary, it was a place to which tradesmen had to bring their weights and scales for periodic inspection. It turned out to be neither one nor the other, but the depot where in the days of trams the electric current was transformed from that used in the city at large to one needed for driving those vehicles. A prosaic explanation, but fact has a charm of its own.

It was a quiet orderly house, with old uniforms, tunics and helmets and framed Victoriana hanging on the walls. I was particularly struck by a nineteenth-century bill announcing a future concert, with *Come into the garden, Maud*, Poetry by Alfred Tennyson, in very small letters, and Music composed by J. C. D. Parker in positively huge ones. It is odd how today's lion is tomorrow's mouse; but perhaps J. C. D. Parker was a local man.

There was a middle-aged chap with a red face and hot blue eyes at the bar, ordering a draught beer that the place did not keep and then crossly demanding if they had a bottle of it 'at least'. The barlady held one up for his inspection, whereupon he fairly screamed, 'Don't shake it! Don't *shake* it!' startling her so that she nearly let it fall. 'Just take the top off,' he continued belligerently, 'and *I* will pour it myself,' which he proceeded to do with a grave total concentration that I thought was only possessed by very small children. He was respectfully watched by three other men and, after the operation was completed and he had taken his first happy pull, a conversation of bewildering complexity sprang up between them, about beers today, beers yesterday, regional beers, national beers, methods of brewing, keeping and drawing, and the great beer drinkers they had known. They were from different classes and parts of the country, one a Scot, one from Lancashire, one too 'posh' for distinguishing regional marks, while he who had set the conference going had Army written all over him, and here they were, drawn into brotherhood by this curious bond. Apart from an odd glass of lager on a very hot day, I never touch the fluid; but, just as Lady Bracknell approved of smoking on the ground that every man needed an occupation, so now I began to hold with beer, since every man ought to have an overwhelming interest. I listened, spellbound, to the astonishing display of knowledge and experience; and the cream of it all was yet to come, for, as they were working up to a crescendo of excitement, a matronly figure appeared and in cool shameless tones called for a beer and lime. 'A' beer, any old beer, and *lime*! A stricken silence fell on the cognoscenti, and they goggled at the blasphemer as if she were barely human.

It does seem wrong to cavil at what is known as Pub Grub, since without it some of us would hardly be able to eat at all; but while they are about it, publicans could easily improve matters in a few very simple ways. There is no need for tired lettuce and flabby tomatoes, let alone for that infamous liquid which comes out of a bottle and which they have the temerity to call mayonnaise. What they serve as ham, too, bears no relation to what civilized people understand by the term, being pallid, slimy and of no recognizable flavour, and as for their 'coffee', I am at a loss to imagine how ever it can be made. When they try their hand at foreign delicacies, the results are more lamentable yet, as for example with *pizza*, anglice 'pectsa', a soggy doughy bun with a smear of cheese

44

and tomato sauce atop, or with *quiche*, which has a kind of soapy custard cradled in a forbidding pastry wall. Both these things are delicious when properly made and, oddly enough, it is no more trouble to make them well than badly: so much so that it looks as if the English either prefer them thus or else are afraid to speak up, lest they be told that no one else has complained. I stuck to the more or less foolproof Ploughman's Lunch; but the other items on offer did wear the same rebarbative aspect to which we have all grown used.

Over this simple rustic meal I studied a few local newspapers, a form of literature that I find absorbing. Much of its interest lies in what is left out and trying to guess how the gaps should be filled is as good as any crossword. Events of a cultural or sporting nature are invariably a great success and the organisers deserving of the warmest thanks, which makes for a good cosy feeling, but you sense that it cannot really have been like that. The trouble is that the reporters know everyone and everyone knows them, and they are constantly running into each other, so that the fearless cut and thrust of Fleet Street is inadvisable.

Another, still graver, problem of theirs is the old one of how to make bricks without straw, efforts to solve which often result in a kind of tadpole item, one with a huge banner headline and precious little tale to follow. And when straw is available in the shape of incest, bestiality or similar old folk customs, it has to be decently processed. There was quite a bale of it in one of the papers now, a father sleeping with his daughter and then aiding and abetting her suicide, which got a brief mention and no headline to speak of at all: the restraint it showed in deference to the solid burghers who would read it, was in marked contrast to the wellnigh Elizabethan ribaldry (I refer of course to the era of Elizabeth I) with which the topic would be bandied about in taverns and other social centres.

How true blue Worcester was appeared in references to its survival as a pocket of 11-plus education in comprehensive Britain. Crafty delaying tactics on the part of Tory councillors had brought this about and now, with the impending election and hoped-for change of government it looked as if Worcester might be safe altogether. The news columns were mainly filled by the minutiae of rural life, however. One fascinating item was headed, Traders Say that Loos Might Be a Tourist Attraction and went on to explain this cryptic utterance: 'New Radnor shortly to be by-passed by the A44 should advertize its as yet unbuilt convenience as a tourist attraction, say the shopkeepers. Facing a loss of income when the by-pass opens, they suggest the provision of conveniences as a way of encouraging tourists to break their journey and visit the town. By a 2–1 majority, a special meeting of electors accepted the suggestion, which has been bandied about in New Radnor for almost 20 years ... ' This little thumbnail sketch was capped by another, revealing that a dearth of signposts in the Wyedean area had led to a stream of complaints and considerable damage to the tourist trade: bold, vigorous measures were advocated also here. A zany strike had been mounted by the dustmen of Wychavon, because their new model dustcart had broken down and had to be replaced for the time being with the old one which they had contentedly used for so many previous years.

I don't think I ever came across any provincial reporters in real life, but I picture them somehow as a careworn melancholy breed of men.

After lunch I went to inquire about transport to Stratford-on-Avon, this being necessary because no one on the local buses ever seems to know anything at all. The range of their ignorance is extraordinary, extending even to such matters as the fares payable on their own line and collected by them every day. Passengers have to stand and wait while they slowly turn over the leaves of a book, for they are reluctant to accept outside advice. It is true that fares are constantly moving upward and have now reached the point where the public prefers to travel by other means or to walk, so that the sight of buses bowling along empty is not uncommon; but one would think that to keep in touch with developments, even if it involved a little mental application, would make their lives just that much more interesting.

The official at the enquiry desk was deep in a personal telephone call, something connected with soccer again, and not to be hurried. Eight minutes went by before he hung up and caught me in the act of consulting my watch.

'Yus?' he demanded, with a nip of frost. 'Stratford-on-Avon? Wrote up on the board, isn't it? Was this morning.'

But I was not going to traipse about the bus station in search of a board, and he finally dug the information up, groaning to himself at the burdens placed upon him. He seemed to think that it was enough to be there, in charge of inquiries, without actually having to answer them: that he was paid not to function but merely to exist. This is an English concept that I had frequently met before, although as a rule among the upper crust of our embassies abroad: at heart, perhaps, he was a Counsellor *manqué*.

Today there was to be one thought-provoking incident after another. On the way back to the hotel I looked in at Debenhams and found the second floor for some reason entirely unstaffed. A number of quite small children, not those redoubtable teenagers for once, were racing about and helping themselves to whatever they fancied, with cries of glee. They were stuffing their loot into capacious plastic holdalls and, seeing me there, taking a friendly interest in them, burst into giggles and made for the stairs. No doubt I should have given chase and put them all under citizen's arrest; but it was really up to the store to do its own police work and I felt that any action by me was bound to turn out badly, perhaps lead to my being lynched by angry mothers.

I had heard of such doings but never witnessed them before. People often spoke as if they indicated a decline or collapse of moral standards, whereas these children struck me as being in a natural state, no more conscious of doing wrong than when they were throwing bricks on to railway lines. Morality is born of fear, alas; no one nowadays frightened them with tales of the bobby or threats of hell. The world was a big delicious oyster and they seemed to be merely in innocent competition as to who could fill his holdall first.

I got back to the hotel to find an accumulation of mail, left in by a friend who had acted as poste restante while I was on the move. The rest of the afternoon had to be spent in writing letters, all of which business had to be attended to against a background of noise from across the river. The quiet, absorbed, fishermen who lined its banks during the week had

47

been replaced by more of the Saturday Goths, who made the welkin ring with their vociferous comments. Everything, I noted, was 'fucking', an all-purpose adjective applied to the rods, the bait, the current, the mud and the absence of a single catch: for what with the row and the steady flailing of lines on the water, the fish had retired in dudgeon. Milton! thou shouldst be living at this hour: England hath need of thee, I mused, as the word fell on my ear again and again, although what the poor man could have done is hard to say.

Presently I went down to dinner. The dining room had a welcome touch of *ancien régime*, the tables attractively laid with shining glass and silver and flowers in little vases. I was the first one there, and made for a place beside a bow window which looked out over the garden. At once a waiter hurried up to say that it was reserved for the boss himself, which I found quite in order. Why keep a hotel at all, if you are not to have the best of everything? I remembered an excellent bistro in Paris where I used to lunch every day and where the practice was faithfully observed. The first time I used the establishment I ordered a pear for dessert and the *patron*, who was also cook and waiter, told me there was none. 'Then what is that?' I asked, indicating a beautiful ripe Comice put carefully aside. '*Celle-là*,' he replied, '*est pour moi.*' And now I sat in a remote corner, befitting my lowly status, and watched the great man when he appeared, a genial portly figure in a colourful waistcoat, with a white moustache that curled over his rosy cheeks in flowing arabesques, like those the Battle of Britain pilots used to wear. Perhaps he had been one of them, and thus deserved his privileges all the more: certainly he looked every inch a landlord in the old tradition, well able to run a cheerful merry house while keeping the guests in their place.

By the time I had finished eating, the Goths had gone and the peace which followed seemed doubly peaceful. There was an open verandah beside the bar, and here I sat, listening to the drowsy cheep of birds and the soft ripples of jumping fish as night came on and stars began to appear. By and by, however, three girls and a bearded youth took a table beside me and began a lively, indeed an impassioned, conversation about the price of everything. Meat had gone

48

up thrice in a week! Steak was outrageous, lobster fantastic, vegetables unbelievable! Nothing whatever was to be had for less than a pound a pound! And what about those mountains of beef and butter, and those lakes of surplus wine that you were always reading about? Enough to make you sick. It was curious talk for such young people, all of whom looked very well fed, while the quiet beauty of the night, which they could enjoy free of charge, went unnoticed. And later on, after they had left, still chattering like fretful monkeys, another of Brian's little outings went by with unearthly screams and groans from the disco and a muffled roar from the ship's engines. Where oh where in the modern world is tranquillity to be found? In the heart of the Sahara desert, maybe.

Chapter Six

Rain was falling in a businesslike manner when I awoke next day, beating on the windowpanes with a sizzle of frying fish. The amiable woman who brought up the newspaper and breakfast tray said it had no intention of leaving off and advised me to stay in bed. It was where she would be herself if she had my luck and Worcester under the rain was nothing to get half-drowned for. But it was Sunday and Mass, like a dog, brings even a comfort-lover out in all weathers.

At least one could take a taxi to church, which would hardly do if a dog was to be exercised, and the rain itself was not too bad by the standards I was used to. The streets were clear of Goths at present but woefully bedraggled by the litter they had left behind them: the cabby described it as a proper disgrace, throwing an empty cigarette box out of the window as he did so. Unlike the young man at Chester he seemed to enjoy his work and take a friendly interest in his fares, for he told me that St George's, which I had asked for, was no great shakes of a place and RC too, and I would be better off in the Cathedral.

St George's was no great shakes indeed, ugly as Jesuit churches so often are, and with its plain glass windows and chandeliers suggestive of a converted ballroom. Less true to Jesuit form was the sermon, as laboured and dull as that of any country parish priest. I am always tickled to hear men complacently quoting Samuel Johnson on women preachers – sometimes the only dictum of his that they know – as if they themselves did better. Without going all the way with Trollope, who devoted some fine invective to contemporary sermons, describing them as the 'scourge of the age', one must admit that on the whole they are a penance. A dog dancing on its hindlegs might really be preferable, offering at any rate some comic relief, while a feeble homily has nothing to recommend it at all. In the days before Vatican II it was even worse, coming as a crude interruption to the beauty of the Old Rite, almost as a deliberate act of vandalism: now the Mass itself has been dragged down to a level where this is hardly felt. There was a crumb of comfort today in our tormentor being an Englishman, uttering his banalities in the Queen's English instead of a rich bog brogue as happens more often than not; but I very soon switched off and gave myself up to secular thoughts of my own.

Despite the predictions of the chambermaid, the rain had stopped by the time that Mass was over, and a walk was possible if not altogether inviting. There were still few people about, no life, no movement, nothing to watch, the very restaurants as firmly shut as the shops and offices, the whole place sunk in Sabbath gloom without even the Salvation Army to liven it up. The English Sunday of peace and quiet is a delightful affair when you have a house and garden in which to savour it, but it does come hard on a traveller. I saw myself back at the hotel, devouring the Sunday paper, advertisements and all, and even, resource of the frantic, going to work on a crossword.

On the way there, however, after a cheerless expensive lunch at the Gifford, I had an unexpected and amusing encounter. A woman in a carefully tended garden outside a trim little villa saw me admiring her flowers and after some talk about them and inquiries regarding myself asked me in for a cup of tea. The room she led me into corresponded to the exterior as far as neatness and cleanliness went but was full of terrible china and glass objects in which she obviously took great pride. What struck me too were the photographs of her husband, a source of even greater pride, indeed of a hero-worship that was most engaging. She wished I could have met him but, a verger at the Cathedral, he was seldom in on a Sunday and we had to make do with his innumerable pictures. Most showed him in full verger's fig, smirking beside some distinguished visitor to the Cathedral, a black world heavyweight champion, for instance, or the Archbishop of Canterbury; but he was also to be seen in evening attire, or a natty suiting with a straw boater to one side on his head, or cycling kit, for he was a dedicated cyclist

51

and promoter of that sport. He was a cocky little bantam with the moustache of an earlier epoch, twisted and waxed into a spike at each end, and an air of much importance.

That there were grounds for this appeared from what his wife had to say of his duties at the Cathedral. The doings there were quite extraordinary, putting Kilvert and Lewis, and for that matter the Arabian Nights, in the shade. Why, only the other week a poor old lady was resting herself on a low wall in the Close when one of these motorbike boys came up and calmly urinated over her. And there were manifold other outrages that her husband was called on to deal with, apparently single-handed. Every night before the Cathedral was shut, he'd go round with his stave looking for the miscreants who hoped to be locked in and wreak all manner of harm: he would find them under pews or in the organ loft or goodness knew where and fearlessly drive them out. All these and similar adventures she recounted with a wifely trust in their authenticity which warmed my heart.

She had experiences of her own as well, for she took in lodgers and you could never tell how they might turn out. There was a woman in just now who had had the nerve to check the house's respectability with the police before she came. 'And we are church people!' When she arrived, she demanded that the cat be kept away from her, as she could never abide a cat. Then she grumbled because there was no key to her bedroom door, and had complained at breakfast of not having closed an eye all night for fear of intruders. The house was in one of the quietest little streets in Worcester, itself no hotbed of crime, but there, my hostess sighed, 'you get them funny sometimes.'

I dropped in at the Cathedral after this to have a look at the hero in person and found him even smaller and cockier than he had appeared in the photographs.

By now the rain had come on again with fresh spirit and there was nothing for it but a return to the hotel, to the newspaper or television. The friendly little dogs, bored with staying indoors, made a rush at me as I came in, snarling fiercely. One of the girls in Reception called out that there was no need to worry, for they never bit anyone, and the other put in 'Except Number 5' which evidently was a standing joke for they both went off into fits of giggles.

The paper was full of election news and commentaries and Mrs Thatcher. Something weird seems to happen to male journalists in England when they write of a woman in public life: now they indulge in an awful coyness of the 'Dare I say it?' or 'If a mere man may venture . . .' sort, now they exhort and advise her from heights of their own imagining, now they dwell on matters that are wholly irrelevant, her voice perhaps, her hair-do or her clothes, where a man would get off scot-free. Standing near a Labour leader at the Magna Carta celebrations in St Paul's, I observed that his shoulders were snowy with dandruff; but when I mentioned this riveting fact to a hawk-eyed political columnist he had not even taken it in. Now, today, another was describing Mrs Thatcher's 'costume', as he quaintly called it, of blue and trimmed with a contrasting 'shade'. No one else revealed the colour of Mr Callaghan's suit or how it was trimmed and readers were left to make what they could of his speech without this helpful pointer. Fleet Street is a bit of a chauvinist pigsty on the whole and it may be done to disparage, to suggest that a woman's appearance is what chiefly matters about her; but it rather makes the writer himself look foolish, especially as he seldom gets the details right.

There were other items of human interest that evening, as good in their way as that of the verger's wife. I was once again first in the dining room and the Italian waiter greeted me with all the warmth of his race as an old and valued friend; and when it transpired that I knew the little town of Camogli, from which he sprang, his enthusiasm overflowed and he treated me to the story of his life. One of a large family, poor but honest, *per Bacco* how honest! he had come to England to seek his fortune and never regretted it: the climate did not trouble him at all, the money was lovely, the people were lovely, and as for our social system, of which he displayed an astounding grasp, and its benefits to himself and family, which he recounted with an endearing child-like candour, there was nothing to touch it in all the world. Here, however, the Boss made a stately entrance and the flood of memoirs dried up.

53

The second happening that night was very strange, and mystifies me to this day. I became the involuntary audience to a private, in fact an intimate, conversation between two men, one of whom had decided on divorce. It took place in the open lounge above the river, where I was listening enjoyably to the sound of rain beating down, delighted to have it all to myself. In came the pair, dressed in good dark suits with quiet ties and polished shoes, clean shaven, hair nicely cut and brushed, the very models one would have said of the discreet, reserved, buttoned-up Englishman, so that the first words uttered in faultless accents came as a distinct surprise.

'God, what a fool I've been!'

'No, no.'

'But yes. An absolute fool. Every one knew but me.'

'Often the way old man.'

'But how could I have been so blind? Looking back, the thing stuck out a mile.'

As far as they were concerned, I might have been invisible. The wronged husband now went into full and fascinating detail of how discovery was made, of what he said to his erring wife and of her memorable reply.

'Not a bit ashamed. Cool as a cucumber. "All right, it's a cop," she said: "Just piss off, mate, and get lost."'

'Nice way for a lady to talk.'

'Well, of course, she was pretty well pissed herself.'

This, I thought to myself, is not the England I knew. There was no accounting for the pair in the scheme of things that I remembered. They were not of that upper crust that is simply unaware of other people's existing. Still further were they removed from that cheerfully low stratum who feel themselves invisible and inaudible whenever they would like to be, the cavorting proles of London parks and Mediterranean beaches. They were somewhere in the middle, not quite of the deprecating kind who apologize if anyone treads on their toes, but certainly careful not to offend. Was it the Telly which had wrought this important change, by constantly dragging people in front of the camera to bare their souls to the million? Or did it come from working in a glass box instead of a private office, open to the gaze of every random passerby? Was the English reserve a thing of the past? I retired from the scene to ponder the case at leisure and, all in all, I felt that I had not done too badly for a rainy Sunday in a provincial city.

English weather is apt to cheer up after a wet weekend when people have to go back to work, and the next day was fine. I spent an agreeable morning in the Shambles and the little streets that ran off it. It is short and narrow and runs parallel with the main street of the city, behind the big chain stores that stand there in a row. I have come to detest these places, with their threatening placards about thieves and prosecution and their snoopers, to whom everyone is an object of suspicion until he has paid up and gone. The barbarous system of self-help was intended to lower costs and so bring prices down but, like so many schemes for human betterment, it has had an opposite effect. What is known as shrinkage, and is merely pilfering, by staff as much as by shoppers, cost the firms millions of pounds every year, a loss they hand on to us: and what with that and wages for security guards and detectives, they might as well employ a staff to serve us in a decent oldfashioned way. The number of normally blameless people who are caught in the act of making off with their goods is not at all surprising: indeed, these impertinent notices fairly ask for it.

But in Worcester one can use them as a short cut and hurry straight through, neither buying nor stealing, to the pleasant old family shops at the rear and the market. As I did this now, I happened to see a consignment of 'lard', imported from the United States as if we had no pigs of our own; whereas the first thing to catch my eye in the Shambles was a little pork butcher with genuine pigleaf in the window from which the finest lard is made, all fresh and free from 'additives' and half the price of the packed American muck in the store.

The queue at this little shop spilled out for quite some way along the pavement. Inside, the jovial proprietor entertained the customers with a flow of chat, leaning comfortably against the wall while his lady assistant put their orders up with rapid nimble movements. I went to the doorway to hear what he said and found that he was bemoaning the state of the nation in no uncertain terms. 'Misery, depression, despair,' he declaimed, 'funny how you never see a smiling face these days ...' His audience was fairly wreathed in smiles, whether because his diatribes were a familiar joke or from the national taste for gloom and disaster, I could not say.

Freshness is the keynote of all the foodshops here: the fishmongers sell what is called now 'wet' fish, to distinguish it from the dry, frozen lumps of tasteless stuff selling in their giant neighbours. They are homely places too, where you still see the blue and white striped aprons and straw boaters of the trade, and where the shopmen are friendly, knowing many of their customers by name. It is also a district for people who know what's what, for even in the market there are provisions of an exotic kind, beautifully dressed crabs, squids, mussels, and all kinds of foreign cheeses, some of them little known, from which morsels are cheerfully cut off for you to try, no matter how expensive they may be. Everyone was taking pains to serve the customer well and, if what he wanted was not available, advice was freely given as to what other place might have it. This seemed to be true not only of the victualling shops, with their regular trade, but those selling boots and shoes, glass and china, riding and fishing tack, birdseed and dog biscuits. Perhaps the reason they keep afloat is that they preserve the personal touch, realizing that good manners mean good business, which is not a copybook maxim but a fact of commercial life.

Here and there were quaint little businesses with somewhat highfalutin names, hinting at a poetic streak in the owners. There was a House of Beautiful Shoes, and a bakery whose bread was 'baked with loving care', and a wine lodge with the mystifying title of *Cellar Vie*, which I concluded must be a corruption of *C'est la Vie*; and stranger still, a clothes boutique which went by the name of *Déjà Vu* and which I could not account for at all, unless the clothes were somebody's cast-offs. Health shops there were, selling ginseng, honey, prunes, senna, herbal tonics and blood fortifiers, a curious phenomenon somehow with all these sturdy apple-cheeked men and women milling about all round them. One notable lack, however, was anything like a real bookshop, the word 'book' denoting a magazine, to be sold along with greeting cards and confectionery; but that was merely a sign of the times, no doubt, and part of a national trend.

And there were various little repair shops too, which came as a pleasant surprise in these days when the idea is to persuade us to throw everything away and get something new. One of them was a cobbler's run by two men in old leather aprons, a sort of Mutt and Jeff pair, one tall and thin, the other short and stocky, and both excellent conversationalists. I went in to ask if they could attend to the heel of one shoe then and there, which they said they most certainly could. The shelves of their dusty room were piled with boots and shoes in every degree of decay and disintegration, but the moment a customer came in to collect his own these were promptly whipped out from among the rest, with the price chalked on the sole: no system, no records were needed, just mother wit and faultless memory. Heaven knows how that couple kept up, for they charged next to nothing.

Another encounter I had that morning was less agreeable. I had been asking for grapes in the market and was told with charming frankness that the only ones in stock were sour. But there was another, high-class, shop in the posh part of the town where better ones could surely be found, and thither I went. Assuming that the friendly civilized ways of the Shambles were local custom, I innocently helped myself to a grape while waiting to be served and this provoked a startling reaction.

'No you don't! None of that!' shrieked a woman whose matted hair put one in mind of a character in Goya's *Dos de Mayo*. 'Just you leave them grapes alone!'

At the price she was charging, I had rather wanted to know what they were like. 'I intend to buy some,' I told her pacifically.

'I dessay ... If everyone carried on like that!'

'Agin the law!' barked a male colleague, a swarthy lad with beetling brows.

'If you did that in Woolworth's, you'd get pinched!' shrilled a shopper.

'I never deal at Woolworth's, madam,' I said with provoking calm.

'Agin the law!' the fellow insisted, although he looked anything but law-abiding himself.

He probably had a legal point, as the grapes worked out at over two pence each; and furthermore the one I took came from a row in the front of the box while those the woman weighed for me, from the back, seemed to be their poor relations. Nevertheless, I had gone there meaning to buy a good deal more, so that they would have done better to say nothing. And as I left the shop a mildly spoken individual was asking if there was any asparagus, to which the reply came pat: 'Yus, but it'll be too dear for *you*.'

The poor man came out after me like a scalded cat. Evidently, these people were their own worst enemies, and certainly they were not at all typical.

As I turned into the High Street, a banging and a caterwauling met my ears and a number of youths came dancing along, accompanied by one depressed-looking middle-aged black. They had the shaven head and yellow robe of Buddhist monks which went oddly with their Saxon features, and they chanted at the top of their voices in a foreign tongue to an accompaniment of drums and tambourines. As no one in Worcester was likely to understand their gibberish, their probable aim was merely to attract attention to themselves; but if so it failed most dismally, as no one so much as threw them a glance. There were no disapproving looks or shaking of heads, the honest burghers seemed to be wholly unaware of their presence, and this was strange as even in London they would have been conspicuous. In fact I found it so strange that I asked a woman what they were at, and she replied vaguely that they were religious. On and on they capered and banged and bawled, right up to the statue of Elgar which faced the memorial to the fallen of the South African War outside the Cathedral: here they paused to catch their breath and recruit their powers before setting off up the High Street again with the same ear-splitting noise, to the same tranquil indifference of the crowd and under the incurious eye of a bobby.

One has to beware of jumping to conclusions when the setting is unfamiliar, of guessing at the whys and wherefores of a happening whose explanation may be perfectly simple.

Perhaps these youths carried on like this so often that they had become a part of the daily round. But as a newcomer I found it very reassuring and all of a piece with the quiet, unworried, amiable spirit of Worcester itself, an ancient city which had seen many queer things come and go. It fitted in with the pleasant impressions left by my morning promenade. And as I turned in the direction of the hotel, the Cathedral began calmly playing a hymn tune on its bells, which fitted in nicely too.

Chapter Seven

At Callow End a few miles from Worcester is Stanbrook Abbey, one of the large Benedictine houses of England, which was my next port of call. I had come to know it some years before, quite by a happy chance. Talking to Iris Murdoch about *The Bell*, a novel that I much admired, I found that she had got the idea for it while visiting 'Lucy', a friend from undergraduate days in Oxford, who subsequently had taken the vows and become Sister Marian O.S.B. There was a guesthouse, described in the novel as The Halfway House, and I booked myself in there without delay, curious to see the place which had fired a novelist's imagination and little suspecting what in time it would also mean to me.

Naturally I was agog to meet this woman of whom Iris had so many delightful stories to tell, some of a none too monastic nature. I amused myself on the journey trying to picture a person whom they would fit, and got it all very wrong. Soon after my arrival at the Hermitage a small figure came flying down the path that led from the Abbey to greet me. A 'silvery' voice, one with that sweetness of silver instruments, bade me welcome in a soft foreign accent but perfect English idiom. A pale heart-shaped face with eyes wide apart, Russian cheekbones and a delicate, far from Russian, nose went with the black and white Benedictine head-dress as if designed for it. She was like a Portrait of a Nun by Velasquez, too much humour and life for El Greco. Iris had prepared me for nothing of this sort. We were friends in a matter of minutes and have remained so ever since.

I was therefore breaking no fresh ground by coming here now, nor would there be any of those significant changes that I was looking for everywhere else. In spite of Vatican II it would be much as it always had been, a centre of activity, edification and, it should be added, amusement. It was also far removed from the idea that people often have of religious houses and thus seems worthy of description. And then, despite a long exile in France, following the suppression of the monasteries by Henry VIII, and its world-wide contacts and the cosmopolitan atmosphere within, it is as thoroughly English a place as could be. That this is not wholly fortuitous appears from a note in the 'Sketch of its History, 1625–1925' by one of the Order, to the effect that in the days of their exile they had from the first been preserved by the care of English monks from the dangerous doctrines that had found their way into too many French convents. What these doctrines were, unfortunately, is not specified: possibly those emanating from Port Royal; but it was clear that the foundation took pride in its immunity from lax foreign thought.

The first *gîte* abroad was at Brussels in 1595. Then in 1622 the nuns acquired a house in Cambrai, whose friendly archbishop granted their request to be under Benedictine jurisdiction. They moved there on Christmas Eve in 1623, and remained for a century and a half. There were twelve of them, 'as fine dames as I have seen and virtuous souls,' said their patron, Dom Rudesind Barlow, and with fine rotund names as well, such as Pudentiana Deacons, Viviana Yaxley, Frances Gawen and Catherine Gascoigne.

They followed the Benedictine Rule of intellectual and manual work alternating, were noted for strict observance and zeal for the Office; they opened a school for children, worked beautiful embroideries, did calligraphy and translated spiritual books from and into the French. Dame Agnes More translated the 'Delicious Entertainments of the Soule' by Francis de Sales, Prince-Bishop of Geneva, with this engagingly candid note at the beginning: 'Know that the printer was a Wallon who understood nothing of English, and the translatress a woman that had not much skill in the Frenche.'

Then came the Revolution. In 1790 the Civil Constitution of the Clergy created schism in the Church in France, with the 'trendies' plighting their troth to the new order, the conservatives staunchly resisting. Two years later the Terror broke out and lasted until Robespierre was himself guillotined in 1794. The nuns suffered greatly, hounded from their Abbey and in constant danger of execution, a fate the Carmelites of Compiègne actually met. After many hardships, sometimes mitigated by unlooked-for kindness from privately sympathetic officials, they reached England in 1795, penniless, exhausted, with nothing but the garments in which they stood, plain clothing given them by the Carmelites before these were martyred.

After various makeshifts, helped by the monks and benevolent laymen, they acquired Salford Hall in Warwickshire, but it was not really what they needed; and in 1836 they bought Stanbrook, described as a house 'pleasantly situated on a lawn, tastefully adorned with fullgrown evergreens and ornamental shrubs; it is approached by a carriage drive and being on an eminence is remarkably dry and healthy.' It also had 'a very genteel Residence,' called the Moat House, with Cider Mill, Coach House, yard and stabling for three horses, a Farmyard, and 25 acres of 'rich Pasture, Orchardings and arable land in a high state of cultivation.'

I have never been happy about the way in which this desirable property was obtained. The nuns felt that 'bigotry was still so strong that it would have been imprudent to deal with the owner in their own name', and accordingly one Dom Bernard Short was asked to act for them. He was 'a handsome man, and well fitted to play the part of a country gentleman. Arrayed in a bottle-green coat, booted and spurred, he rode up to Stanbrook Hall and asked to be shown over the property. Mr Thompson (the owner) received him very pleasantly and conducted him through the house and grounds. Fr Bernard made particular inquiries about the shooting and hunting in the neighbourhood, and showed great anxiety about the wine-cellars . . .'

Mr Thompson was delighted to find so suitable a purchaser and the deal went through. Some time later, however, he espied Dom Bernard in clerical garb at an auction and inquired agitatedly as to who he might be. On learning the truth he expressed himself with vigour, but there was nothing now to be done.

Thus Stanbrook was acquired by means of what can only be described as a barefaced confidence-trick. I put this once to a member of the community, as saintly a being as I have known, and she replied in all seriousness, 'but otherwise we should never have got it.' I fear that this simple approach to matters may have had something to do with the bigotry which the nuns apprehended, and that while they felt they were doing the Lord's work, in Mr Thompson's eyes they were nothing but slippery popish frauds. It looks as if a little of France had rubbed off on the holy women after all. Still, that is water under the bridge by now, and certainly it is agreeable to think of Dom Bernard, disguised in his green coat and tall boots, prattling away of pheasant and fox and the proper conditions for keeping wine. And let us hope Mr Thompson got some of his own back by spreading the news of how particular the nuns were about their claret.

Today, the Abbey is much as described on the 19th-century bills, with a commodious church added. As the Order is enclosed, I had never set eyes on more of it than may be seen from the small public chapel beside the Sanctuary with a grille between: namely, the entrance through which the nuns file in from their cloister, a few front stalls and the organ above them. Once when the Sanctuary grille was still drawn back after Mass I asked the Sacristan if I could take a pace or two forward and get a glimpse of it, and she replied with a beaming smile, 'Certainly you may not.' There is nowhere like Stanbrook for good straight answers.

The mighty cedars outside must be the 'fullgrown evergreens' also referred to, but there are other trees, including a magnificent copper beech; and from the enclosed part of the grounds in summer time comes the waft of scented poplar. Cheeky little grey squirrels frolic about by day, and the night is full of the demented shriek of owls. The garden never seems to be quite without flowers, the last autumn ones hardly gone before snowdrops, jasmine and aconite appear: I remember Fr Dominic the chaplain pointing to a clump of Honesty and remarking 'strange to see that'. It was indeed rather early; but he went blandly on, 'In a monastery garden, I mean.'

Bells give some idea of what is going on within, the first being the rising one at five, followed at somewhat erratic hours by the Angelus. For years the Stanbrook version of this has fascinated me, but I have never got to the bottom of it. The orthodox ring is three pulls of three with a pause between each, and then a steady pull of nine. Stanbrook gets the three pulls of three all right, but thereafter apparently is carried away: I have lain in bed, shaking with laughter, and counted up to forty-two. Not all the village people who live within earshot are so much amused. Another of Stanbrook's little departures is the gay carillon before High Mass on Sunday, forbidden to Catholic places of worship by law: they are supposed to know their place and summon the faithful with a subdued kind of tolling. And there is the Passing bell, which I have never heard, when a nun is on the point of death.

Those who come to the Abbey to visit relations or friends, or on business, or to sit at the feet of the nuns, are received in the parlours. The word brings a thought of chintz and potted flowers and a paper fan across the grate in summer, but in fact derives from the *parloirs* of French convents; and formerly the nun was shielded from worldly contact by a massive grille surmounting a wooden table that ran from wall to wall. Then the grille was whipped away, as contrary to the spirit of the age, but the room left otherwise as it was, bare and spare in the Benedictine style. Then this also was apparently thought too forbidding, and the parlours were divided into smaller compartments, furnished with little tables and plastic chairs. Flower arrangements in the spirit of Constance Spry began to appear and a genteel cosiness now prevails. This development fills some of the community with innocent pride, and a frequent question was, 'What do you think of the new parlours?' I could not abide them, but perhaps I have been too much in Spain, where austerity and formality survive and the grille in no way inhibits conversation, rather the reverse.

However, surroundings are soon forgotten in the pleasure of talking to the nuns. Young and old, they are as merry and clever a bunch as one could hope to meet. Many have special gifts or accomplishments: the Mistress of Music plays the organ exquisitely, there is a painter known far beyond the monastery walls, a Master Printer of equal renown, scholars in various fields, some of whom undertake literary or editorial work for secular bodies, all bringing in revenue for the House. When not occupied with these, or engaged in prayer or meditation, they carry out the chores, cook, sew, scrub, garden, do plumbing or repairs, or look after poultry. The BBC wanted to make a programme of the Abbey once but leave was not granted for, as Lady Abbess observed, there is no filming the contemplative life and the rest is merely external. On the other hand, an author did spend a long time there, industriously gathering material for a book, noting rules, traditions, customs, and getting every assistance; but the result in my opinion was lamentable. The author used this load of accurate detail as the background to a story of her own contriving and, concerned to show that nuns were human beings, had some of them up to all sorts of improbable deeds. Human they certainly are, thank goodness, but in a Roedean kind of way, if I may so express it. Tell me that Dame X biffed Dame Y with a broom and, with a violent effort of the imagination, I might just believe it; but plotting and listening at doors are simply out. Iris Murdoch did far better in *The Bell*, which one of the community who was at Oxford with her, while deploring her *oeuvre* in general, praised for its insights into the religious life. But it takes one of Miss Murdoch's gifts to draw these truths from the air and find the means to convey them. I can only speak of the sense of refreshment and renewal which time spent at the Abbey has always brought me. When people ask, as they sometimes do, 'But what good are they?', short of rudely replying 'And what good are you?' I cannot think of much to say; but at least I do know.

A consequence of being here is that the world and its wag seem not only far off but somehow unreal. Now we were just coming up to the General Election and it was interesting how the doings of various public figures, which I had previously followed with respectful attention, took on the zany inconsequence of a Punch and Judy show. For example, there was Mr Michael Foot with a characteristic squib on how not to win co-operation with the government in the fight against inflation: 'you cannot do it by force, you cannot do it by shooting people ...' Then up popped Mr Whitelaw: 'Who are these people the Government is going to shoot? I would like to know how he justifies that in any way. I hope he won't say any more about shooting people . . . ' Then Mr Foot came back, forecasting a 'maniac government' in power, to renewed protests from Mr Whitelaw. These statesmanlike exchanges had me in fits of laughter. I could just see Mr Whitelaw leaning out of his box and demanding, 'Am I right, children?' or raining blows of his truncheon on Mr Foot's subversive head; but of course both gentlemen were wholly in earnest.

Nevertheless, although politics are rarely mentioned here, on polling day the entire community turned out to vote, leaving the enclosure by special dispensation. The green landscape of early summer was speckled by black habits and white wimples as they walked down by twos and threes, obviously enjoying the adventure. Many that I knew by name and fame but had never seen before I now met on the road, beaming with innocent pleasure; but every time I passed a group a strange thing happened, as if the Fiend himself were taking a hand in it. For, since a Conservative victory by now was clearly in the bag, I had gone to the Pound shop to lay in a bottle or two for the purposes of celebration; and while these held their peace as long as I walked alone, no sooner did I meet the nuns than they gave a disloyal derisive clink, covering me with confusion and drawing smiles of sympathy from the holy women.

The oldest of these had been taken down by car, and I afterwards heard that some had felt bewildered and hardly known what to do, although with reluctance I discount a mischievous allegation that one of them had written *Nihil obstat* against her candidate's name. It is a fact, however, that Dame Mary came toddling out of the booth to know if she should put a line through the names she did not fancy, or what. The night before she had confided to me that she was a Tory, with a revelatory air as if, left to myself, I must have assumed she was a Trotskyite: so it was as well that she did not spoil her paper, for a vote is a vote after all, even in what might be about the safest seat in England. She was delighted with the result when it came through, although somewhat mystified at first by the name of Thatcher: I don't know what she had been expecting, unless it were Disraeli.

I have had many a Parlour with Dame Mary, in one of the

old-fashioned survivors if we can get it: it is a treat to look forward to as, in her words, we have always hit it off. The key turns in the lock of the door dividing the world and the *clausura*, and the small figure comes in, murmuring 'Deo Gratias'. Her father was a Judge in India, and her youthful experiences were chiefly of that country, France and Lausanne, where she went to school. In the first World War she served as a VAD at Dunkirk, but did not like it as she was kept out of harm's way to the rear and she wanted to be 'in the scrum': so she transferred to a Quaker unit and, in one of their ambulances, was shelled to her heart's content.

The saga of her war work is one of her 'set pieces,' as novel-reviewers call them, and she tells it repeatedly, to my great satisfaction. People who fret if they hear the same thing more than once, however good, always puzzle me; and I have noticed that they are often the kind whose own remarks hardly need making at all. Another Marian set piece I much enjoy is the story of how she came to Stanbrook, a real *coup de foudre*. Some occasion had brought her there as a visitor, when still in her teens, and she knew at once that she belonged to it. She was the child of a mixed marriage, her Catholic father dead and her Protestant mother loyally bringing her up in the Faith, as she had undertaken to do; but the last thing she had envisaged or could approve was that her ewe lamb might take the veil.

At twenty-one, however, Dame Mary could resist the call no longer. She quietly left her mother's house and took the evening train to Paris ('It leaves Lausanne at seven o'clock, you must of course know it', this being merely fifty odd years ago) crossed to London and took the train from Paddington to Worcester, which went at ... at ... oh. DRAT me –

'Three o'clock,' I prompted her.

Three o'clock, that was it, and on to Stanbrook by taxi. She gave the driver what money she had left, an enormous tip, and notified a startled Lady Abbess that she wished to enter.

'No *glamour*, all very matter-of-fact.'

She had been fortunate in her novice mistress and a strong affection grew up between them, which her superiors did not disapprove although, in a general way, particular friendships seem frowned upon in the monastic life. I told her once that I

67

should find this the hardest part of it, this equally well-disposed feeling to all and sundry, and she replied at once, briskly, 'Well you haven't been called to it, have you?' her face lighting up with the sudden small-boy grin that is a characteristic.

It is indeed a mysterious business, that peremptory call that is not to be gainsaid, sooner or later must be answered, frequently causing heartache, or heartbreak, to the family and friends who look on helpless and uncomprehending. Dame Mary never looked back, had no doubts or regrets, and today is one of the best-loved women in the community, as well as a source of anxiety to it. Her memory is not what it used to be, except for matters of long ago, and she is apt to wander about, trying to think where she ought to be and what doing. When first I knew her, she had a disconcerting habit of rising in the middle of a Parlour and hurrying off without a word, to carry out some pressing duty which existed only inside her brain: presently she would return, remarking contentedly, 'Well, I've settled *their* hash.' She has given that up now, but the community keeps a sharp look-out for her, since she was found half-throttled by the cord of her veil which she was attempting to tie for herself.

Still, the affectionate description of her, once given me by the then Mother Prioress, 'completely gaga', I must strongly deny. She often comes out with very shrewd or pointed remarks, not always in strict conformity with doctrine. I remember when we somehow got on to marriage laws in the Greek Orthodox church, and I said how odd it seemed that you might divorce twice, or lose two spouses by death and re-marry once, but a third marriage could not be allowed, whichever way the others had ended.

'Well, it is nice to know they all get a chance,' Dame Mary said, after thinking it over.

One of her set pieces gave me a good deal of trouble, although of an interesting kind. It concerned a haunted house in the neighbourhood, wellknown for its size and its ghost, a ferryman who would drown his richer passengers in the river that runs near by and then bring their bodies indoors to despoil them. He was supposed to make himself heard at night, dragging the corpses upstairs. And not so long ago a skeleton was actually found here, walled in, dressed in the uniform of a Cavalier officer, as could be seen from the buttons on the tunic. The house had often changed hands, because of the ghostly disturbances, until a rakehelly crowd took it on and made such a racket that the ghost took to its heels. Indeed, if anyone is plagued by a ghost, he might do worse than open a disco.

Well, I thought I would investigate this house and amuse Dame Mary with a first-hand account of it, but it was easier said than done. In fact, I learned more of contemporary village life than anything else. The building was said to be down a lane opposite one of the village pubs, about half a mile or so, but no one there, neither the landlord nor a customer, knew the present owner's name or anything of the story. Then I walked down the lane itself, asking the people I met, not one of whom could tell me a thing. They were not of the village at all but mere commuters, working in Worcester or even Birmingham, sitting of an evening in their bungalows or villas, watching the tele as it wandered about the globe, with no interest whatever in local affairs.

I do not know how many people I asked or books I consulted before the facts came out. The house was called Prior's Court, and had belonged to Malvern Priory until Henry VIII seized it for a favourite of his, after which it descended privately from hand to hand and only came on the market in quite modern times. It stood to one side of the village near the river and was approached by a drive with tall trees, including a magnificent copper beech such as one often finds in this part, and many daffodils blowing. To one side, near the courtyard, was a real cock-pit, a large scoop out of the earth like a miniature Devil's Punch Bowl, with the grass that covered it and the surrounding verges all beautifully mown.

I had asked Sister Marian who was an extern, a kind of liaison officer between the monastery and the world, to come along, as with her sweetnesss of manner and charming appearance, not to mention a notable strength of character, she acts as a talisman to get you in wherever you wish to go. We found the owners, a pleasant young couple, busy washing their car, and asked if we might look round a little: they willingly agreed and also invited us in to see a few of the rooms and the chief stairway. It was a delightful building with a great sense of space and solidity and proportion, the chimneys Elizabethan, the rest added in Jacobean style: we did not like to ask what the present owners had in mind but it seemed rather big for a private dwelling today.

The mistress of the house knew nothing of the diabolical ferryman, but had heard tell of three ghosts, all of murdered women, and one of her children had been afraid to sleep in a bedroom at the top of the reputedly haunted stairs. There had never been any manifestation, however, and she put the rumours down to village children's talk. The discovery of the Cavalier officer had been a fact: some sharp-eyed visitor had noted a discrepancy between the outside and the inside of the house, suggesting that a small room at one end had been walled off and the windows bricked in: this had been opened and the skeleton found.

But when I reported back to Dame Mary, she had forgotten about it and I had to go through the entire saga that she had told me herself. Only when I got to the Cavalier's tunic and the special buttons on it did she eagerly interpolate, 'Of solid gold! That's what gave the show away!' After that, she again disclaimed all knowledge of what I was talking about but, her interest roused, begged that I would start at the beginning again and tell her exactly what had transpired.

One of the attractive pitfalls of her conversation is that you never know where you are, or what may be coming next. I believe what happens is that when she appears to be done with a topic or to lose the thread of it, it has merely gone underground, as rivers do, and will presently rise and flow again. One afternoon we were discussing – as I thought – the Monastery cat, said to be broken-hearted by the death of the nun who took care of her. I remarked that it was not in the nature of cats to break their hearts for such a trifle and that, once Pussy found her supplies of milk and fish forthcoming, her heart would rapidly piece itself together.

'But will she have the courage to face the facts of life?' Dame Mary inquired, with a singular earnestness.

I said, most probably she would have to.

'She has courage, we know,' Dame Mary pursued. 'But will she always show it? The great thing is, to open the eyes

70

of the lower orders. It seems that at last they are beginning to open. But will she stick to it, will she face the facts of life and bring them home to the rest?'

I realized then, it was not Pussy she had in mind, but our new Prime Minister. We had been talking about her earlier on. Hardly had I adjusted to this than, slipping easily into French, she recalled one by one the details of her flight from Lausanne to Stanbrook, rounding the story off with a verse from Verlaine, repeated without a mistake.

'But, drat me, I am dull,' she said next. 'You are too patient with me. How can you be so patient?'

I told her, truthfully, there was no one I enjoyed talking to more.

'I know what it is,' she said with her little grin, after a brief meditation. 'You have me down on your Lent Bill! But surely, Lent is over?'

She was referring to the list of penances and mortifications that nuns impose on themselves during Lent, which I had never heard of before. Lent Bill, indeed! I revelled in her. Of all her remarks, my favourite was when I told her I found it easier to converse with Anglican clergy than with our own. 'Well of course, my dear,' she said. '*They* are gentlemen!'

From time to time she would worry a little over what she considered the undue comfort of the Abbey, for instance, the very temperate, indeed all but imperceptible, central heating. 'We, who are vowed to Poverty . . . ' And then a benefactor left the Community a substantial sum on condition that extra bathrooms were installed and the kitchens brought up to date. As far as the latter went, Dame Mary had no grounds for concern, for when the work was completed one of the younger women informed me that the food was just as awful as ever. She obviously thought this an excellent joke. From time to time I had meals in the Abbey itself, instead of the guest-house, and while generous in scale, they undoubtedly are somewhat penitential in flavour: not deliberately so, I think, for Benedictines have never gone in for rigorous mortification – the Rule even allows a measure of wine at every meal, although I have never known it taken in England – but rather resulting from the way in which the House is run. Once a year there is a change of office, when Lady Abbess formally 'deposes' every nun and the Council re-allocates the various duties as seems to it best; and she who is appointed cook may never have fried an egg in her life before, a state of affairs which reveals itself in the product.

Nevertheless, the spirit is willing enough, as I realized when Dame Teresa asked me to translate a recipe she had for one of the more elaborate *paellas*, Valenciana as I recollect. The ingredients alone were staggering, with certain items, such as *cigalas* and *langostinas*, that would probably have to be flown from Spain, special spicy *chorizo* sausages, mussels, chickens, peppers, baby artichokes, tomatoes, peas, rice, saffron at £1.50 a gramme and olive oil at £7 and more a quart. I ventured to suggest that Dame Cellarer might not countenance this. 'But perhaps on a High Feast day?' replied Dame Teresa hopefully. It was not for me to comment further, and I carried out the little task as required; but I did privately wonder what inexpert hands would make of it all, supposing permission were granted. It would be a sorry end to a Feast if the entire Community were laid low.

Dame Teresa came from the West Indies and had all the warmth and gentleness of her Portuguese descent, as well as a great love of fun. She was also clever and well- educated, fit for all kinds of literary work or administration. One day, however, my blood ran cold to hear it seriously proposed that she return to the West Indies, there to establish and edit a newspaper. The mere thought of her struggling helplessly in that alligator tank was appalling. Happily the plan came to nothing, and she set to work on a monumental index of Coleridge's notebooks instead.

There were many interesting and delightful characters in the monastery, all different from each other and few corres-ponding to popular notions of what nuns are or should be like. Parlours with Dame Marcella, an Anglo-Irishwoman who had entered late and previously led a full social life were invariably entertaining and often hilarious: so much so that I was astounded when she left the Abbey to become a hermit. The only hermits of my experience were the gaunt ragged men who formerly spent their days in meditation on the slopes of the Sierra Morena above Cordoba. It was not easy to picture the vivacious Dame in that role and possibly she had her own conception of it, for on departing she begged that Bernard Levin's articles in *The Times* might be preserved and forwarded to her pious retreat.

Yet another charmer was Sister Laurentia, the daughter of an Anglican parson, who after all her long years at Stanbrook seemed to come fresh from some oldworld vicarage. She was Sister, not Dame, being an extern whose duties lay partly outside the enclosure, one of them being to care for the flower garden. In appearance she was a pleasanter version of the Queen in *Alice in Wonderland*, with much the same decided manner of expressing her views. I used to act as under-gardener off and on and it was a privilege to work with her, for she knew a great deal about trees, flowers, birds and all to do with country life. She was a kind but bewildering taskmistress, her ideas and suggestions tumbling out in such eager profusion that for some while after a talk with her I was unable to take in anything that was said to me by her or anyone else. She was also rather a worry, because she went to work as impetuously as a girl and she was neither young nor spry. One blustery morning I found her capering round a bonfire, piling dead leaves and sticks upon it while the flames licked hungrily at the voluminous overall above her habit, and I begged her to be careful: to which she replied with a nip of frost: 'Thank you! I know what I'm doing. Been a countrywoman all my life.' This expertise did not always save her from getting the worst of it while digging out a recalcitrant root or stone: she would pull manfully on her spade until the object unexpectedly rose and she measured her length, supine, her little boots waving in the air. On these occasions she disliked offer of help or anxious inquiry, preferring me to behave as if nothing had happened at all. She died suddenly and calmly one night, and for days afterwards the garden felt extraordinarily full of her presence.

During my present visit, there was an amusing contretemps, or amusing at any rate to an unregenerate worldling, when *The News of the World* telephoned to ask if their reporter might come and have interviews. Lady Abbess had never heard of this organ: she knew *The Times*, which is delivered daily for anyone with leisure to read it, but her acquaintance with the national Press stopped at that, nor has she ever sought publicity. Nevertheless, she gave her assent, leaving it to individuals to decide if they wished to respond. I never found out who broke the news of the paper's reputation, but he or she must have pitched it strong, for there was a considerable to-do and searching of hearts, and the usually smiling Abbess looked very worried and sad.

In fact, the reporter was only after 'human interest' material and colour, putting the harmless questions that might be expected – why did you enter, what did your family say, how did you feel at first, what do you do with your time and so forth – and the 'story' eventually appearing in that often maligned publication was such as would not have been refused the *imprimatur* anywhere. But the incident was revealing of the depths, or rather heights, of innocence prevailing among these women, and also of how quick some people were to judge them. One pious Catholic of the locality remarked to me, she never thought the day would come when Stanbrook sank so low; but I think perhaps she had never read the paper herself, and was speaking from hearsay. Fr Dominic, on the other hand, was entranced by the whole affair, and grinned like a Cheshire cat whenever it came up.

Perhaps I am even wickeder than I imagine, for, like one staying in a mountain resort who occasionally feels a desire for the polluted air of the plain, I would sometimes slip out for a drink in a pub and listen to the untrammelled talk of the locals. There was a burly lorry-driver one evening, explaining how you fiddled a tachometer count by means of a silicon chip, highly technical stuff, far above my head, but quite enthralling. Everyone in the bar felt the same, listening without disapproval or censure but with the keen attention due to facts of scientific and social importance. And at that very moment, not half a mile away, the nuns were chanting Vespers in their sweet song-bird voices. In truth, it takes all sorts to make a world; but the contemplative religious are a very special sort, and the world would be a poorer place without them.

Chapter Eight

I went on from the Abbey to some friends who were lucky in being able to please themselves as to how and where they lived; and as usually happens in such cases they had chosen the country. It is strange that England should have thrown up some of the greatest cities in the world, because there was never a more stoutly rural people. You could really say that inside every English townsman a rustic was struggling to be let out. And it is strange too that our cities should be on the whole so ugly, for few races are more alive to the beauties of landscape, of trees, rivers and hills. Perhaps their rebarbative surroundings are the cause of that gloomy aspect so many townsmen wear, which foreigners take for a national characteristic but which mostly clears up as they put the key in their own front door. At every holiday, however short, there is a wild rush for the countryside or the sea, even if it means inching along for hours, bonnet to tail, in a solid mass of traffic. By the time they reach their destination it is nearly time to start for home again, but no matter. They hurriedly sniff the air, gulp their sandwiches down and reckon the day well spent.

These friends of mine had escaped from the oriental hugger-mugger of Kensington to the delicious environs of Ledbury in Herefordshire. They had bought an old farm and were bringing it to life, building, transforming and planting. While prospecting for a suitable place they had been greatly drawn to Radnor for its wild beauty and untrodden ways but, as they said, 'It mightn't do to be ill there' and they had a small boy to think about. And then, of course, it is pleasant to be able to shop without planning on a veritable safari. So it was Herefordshire, with civilisation not too far away.

The weather, which had been wintry for some time with snow, hail and biting winds from the east now turned over-

75

night, and the countryside was bathed in sun. The great perry trees in the orchard, tall and spreading as trees of the woodland, promptly burst into flower but the apples held back, as much as to say they had been fooled before.

Every time I came here, there was something new to enjoy. Now it was a pond which they had dug, collecting its water from a stream: in the middle was a pile of rushes, on the top of which a moorhen of manic appearance had built her nest, and voles popped into and out of the banks or swam to and fro in the brownish water like busy little clockwork toys. All the work had been done by my friends themselves with the help and supervision, not always to the purpose, of their small son. In fact they do nearly everything themselves except the actual building or carpentry, and in autumn perform the prodigious task of stripping the perry and cider-apple trees, bagging the fruit and hauling it to the presses.

The following day was a Sunday, with an open air agricultural show in the afternoon. There was a charmingly free and easy exhibition of dogs, mostly terriers, but with a few elegant slinky Afghans, friendly Labradors and pink-eyed spotted Dalmatians also to be seen. As usual, the smaller the dog, the greater his importance and self-esteem, and one which looked for all the world like a blowsy chrysanthemum held himself completely aloof, giving only a faint whirr of indignation if anyone dared to address him. There was a gymkhana too, with show jumping and a musical competition, the riders trotting about a space dotted with sacks and, when the music stopped, hurriedly dismounting and racing to the nearest of these. The rules required them to keep on the move, but a high proportion were gaily cheating, circling round and round a sack until the moment came to leap from the saddle and plant a foot on it in triumph, like Royalty with a tiger shot by somebody else.

The highspot of the gathering was a display of ancient farm machinery, laid out on the grass, while the owners sat beside them, some wearing bowler hats such as I have not seen for years. Every machine had a placard beside it announcing its provenance, such as 'Found in orchard, covered with lichen and in poor condition, acquired and restored by Mr A and sold to Mr B', and so on, all of them polished up and in working order, none of them of any conceivable use, but plainly the owner's pride and joy. Young Francis, my friends' son, was enchanted, kept running back and back for another look, and finally was allowed to sit in a 1927 tractor, which crowned his day.

Best of all for me were the three great shire horses, one of them a Suffolk Punch, with a splendid chestnut body, shining like a new conker, and luxuriant mane, which brought memories of my East Anglian childhood. It was so long since I had seen one, I was afraid the mighty breed had vanished. He and the others were in *grande tenue*, their harness heavy with bright brasses, and with red, white and blue cockades affixed to the elaborate ornaments on their heads. I should have liked to find out more about the place of the shire horse in the modern world, and inquired for the relevant Society, since everything in England almost, from goats to homemade jam, has one of these; but Penny, my hostess, said that the only member she knew was *incomunicado*, his wife having put him out of the house and refused to pass on messages.

There was also a raffle with a bizarre assortment of prizes, the more acceptable of which were bottles of spirits or wine. The winning numbers of these, called out, were received with ironic cheers, particularly in the case of a portly gentleman, apparently wellknown in the neighbourhood, whose complexion hinted that this piece of luck had come to the right quarter. Although we ourselves bought tickets in bulk, we won nothing whatever, not even the hideous Chinese vase.

Incidentally, I was surprised to read a few days later that the Revenue was poking its nose into the matter of alcoholic prizes. Those we saw, at least, had been donated by private benefactors, so that duty must at some point have been paid. It appeared that a warped individual, whom the very police had nicknamed Blue Nose, was going about from one of these happy and harmless occasions to the next, denouncing all who offered this kind of attraction; and apparently some fool of a magistrate had upheld him. There is a type of being who can see nothing pleasant without doing his best to stop it; and I hope, I imagine, that the inquiries he set afoot cost a great deal more than they brought in.

In the evening I walked out as far as the Little Marcle church of St Michael, built in 1870 by J. W. Hugall. Of him, Nikolaus Pevsner says in his *Herefordshire*, 'Hugall was evidently one of the naughtier High Victorians', as the church has a bell-turret and crosses on nave, chancel and porch. The way to it led past a beautiful farmhouse and barnyard, the buildings of mellow rosy brick, which looked so attractive in the fading sun that on the walk homeward I felt like going in to ask if I might look round. As I hesitated, nerving myself with Boswell's sound remark, that he would never be deterred by the fear of a snub, an old black dog came out and looked at me thoughtfully, wagging his tail. But it was all so quiet and Sunday evening-ish that I hadn't the heart to knock on the door.

It may have been my guardian angel holding me back, for I heard afterwards that the farmer, who lived alone, would never speak to a woman and no more than need be to a man. Moreover, he was said to keep several dogs who were given to biting people, including those who worked about the place. From another source came the information that if any domestic fowl, duck, chicken, turkey, strayed on to his land he upped and shot it. But legends will always grow in a small community about such people who go their own way. Robin, my host, whose land marched alongside, had never heard a gun fired there at all; and the owner was indubitably a first-rate husbandman, with his fine hedges, sturdy gates, fruit-trees each with a protective shield against bark-nibbling animals, and apple-pie order everywhere.

The next day we all went off to the captivating little town of Ledbury. I had been there before, staying with a friend who was formerly a Master of the local pack, and had gone back on one occasion since, to the Boxing Day Meet. This took place outside the historic Feathers Inn, after which the Hunt cantered once or twice the length of the High Street before setting off; and very splendid traditional types there were among them, purple-faced and tall-hatted, as well as some magnificent horses. Besides being a seasonable event, it was a fund-raising operation and young people were going about collecting, but so politely and discreetly, one hardly knew where they stood.

'I hope you are not Anti,' I remarked to a small boy who shyly held out his box: whereupon what *Punch* used to call a Total Stranger, bearded and scruffy, called out *en passant*, 'I am, as a matter of fact!' and went on looking well pleased with himself, as if he had struck a blow for something. In general, however, the opposition was keeping mum, deterred no doubt by the throngs of farmers and horsey people all round it. Such anti-field sport characters as I have met were of the kind that rates discretion above valour, and I have often wondered if their hatred of the hunting fraternity does not spring from envy of its pluck rather than real concern for the fox. There are far more cruel things done to animals every day which seem to worry them not at all.

After the ride-off came the country dancers, with blackened faces, belled gaiters, fancy waistcoats and breeches and brightly coloured handkerchieves, who flailed the air with cudgels as the Tirolese slap with their hands in the Schuhplättler, but with worse effect if anyone made a miscalculation. They were a real pleasure to watch, for here were no self-conscious folksy revivalists but sturdy youths, performing with more gusto than elegance and making a stronger effect for that very reason.

The town had changed but little, except for a number of small canning and preserving factories that had shot up on the outskirts, unsightly but not too visible; and the end of the village, or Homend, once so well preserved had been somewhat marred by a rash of superstores. As in so many delightful old places, too, houses were being shaken badly by juggernaut lorries. Six roads meet here, linking the county towns of Hereford, Worcester and Gloucester, as well as the ancient ecclesiastical centres of Leominster, Bromyard, Ross, Deerhurst, Tewkesbury and Malvern, and the former inland port of Upton on Severn; and at certain times one really does feel as if the traffic from them all were converging on Ledbury at once. A by-pass is planned and in the Old Market House, begun in 1618 as a Corn Exchange, there was a display purporting to show what the authorities had in mind but in fact consisting of a few vague drawings pinned to boards. In charge of them was a man with a beard – for some reason, beards and planning go together – whose function it was to answer questions. Penny, whom I was staying with, asked if a preservation order had been made for a certain splendid oak standing dangerously near the intended route, but he could not say. It is to be hoped that someone is getting on with the scheme. At the Upper Cross in the High Street, a sixteenth-century timbered house with pillars and overhang had been so beset by lorries unable to turn off comfortably in the space available that the pillars were grazed, the plaster above them knocked off and the warning sign 'overhang' bent to such a degree that lorrymen could hardly have seen it. It was one more sad example of the threat to old treasures that could never be replaced.

We went on to Weston's cider and perry factory, up a drive past cheerful flowerbeds and trim lawns to an invitingly old-fashioned office. Having rung a ponderous handbell, such as calls you to meals or classes at school, we composed ourselves to wait. The room was ringed by musty old barrels, or vats rather, photographs of heaped-up fruit hung upon the walls, and there was a delicious smell of apple in the air. In due course an unhurried man appeared, who bore our cider cask away to fill it and, on returning, offered us a drink of perry from a jar on the desk. I was glad of it, for this was the first warm day of the year, and also I had never tasted perry before. Not only that, but I had never seen it displayed in any pub or heard anyone asking for it. It was very pleasant, quite as good as cider, but afterwards I came on an article in *Herefordshire County Life* which gave a reason for its unpopularity: namely that because of its laxative qualities it could not be drunk on the same scale as cider. It was often said of perry that 'it went round and round like thunder and out like lightning'.

In this same publication there were stories about both drinks, showing the robust, somewhat Germanic, sense of humour that persists in our country folk. One man invited another, with whom he had a crow to pluck, for a game of cards and a glass of cider, which he had laced with jalap, a strong Mexican purge. Soon the unhappy guest began to feel discomfort and kept saying that he must leave; but every time the host dealt again and plied him with more of the dire tipple. At last his victim cried 'I must GO!' and dashed to the door, only to find it locked.

80

In the same issue of this racy print there was an article on the importance of cider by one of a family that had lived 500 years in the area. No man would willingly go to work on a farm where the cider was bad, or where the farmer was reckoned mean about it. One old man, asked how he was fed at his first living-in job, said, 'Not bad at all, a quart of cider on rising, breakfast a bit of bacon, a quart of cider, and fill the bottle up for the morning.' The bottle held two quarts. 'Dinner, a bit of beef, a quart of cider, and fill the bottle: tea, this and that, a quart of cider; supper, a bit of cheese and a quart of cider. Pretty well of cider, wasn't it? Well, I usually had a quart going to bed.'

His daily intake was therefore nine or ten quarts, and this was by no means uncommon.

The description of cider-making also called up visions of a bygone age. The apples were picked in late autumn, mostly by women or gypsies, and pressing began in December. Fruit was placed to begin with in a large round stone trough and a horse was hitched to an upright millstone which ground it to pulp. Horses were very keen on this job, as they were always allowed to lick the stone as the juice began to flow. Crushing went on until the pips burst, when the *must* was carried to the press and all the liquid squeezed out, transferred to casks and allowed to ferment on its own without sugar or yeast. However, certain ingredients of an enriching or fortifying nature were added, beef, blood, raisins, for example. Whatever went in, the cider was consumed and nothing remained when the casks were empty. An old man once declared, the best cask of cider he ever tasted produced the skeletons of several rats when it was being washed out for the next year's brew. It was supposed that the animals had made their way in through the bung-hole while the juice was working. So if we feel inclined to make some ourselves we shall know how to set about it.

Weston seemed a firm entirely after my own heart, but not altogether geared to the pace of modern production. They are said to have, for example, no planting policy. The great perry trees go on for two to three hundred years, but in the end they do need replacing; but Weston does nothing about them, nor about apples. Bulmer, the other great local name, provides farmers with apple-trees and plants them, keeping a friendly eye on them afterwards: not so, Weston. Their transport, too, has a style of its own, they tell me, and should you run across a particularly complicated snarl-up, be it in Knightsbridge, be it in Ledbury, its core may well be a Weston lorry. Nevertheless, their product is delicious and, to my taste, better than that of the provident far-sighted Bulmer.

On our way home we stopped at the kindergarten to pick young Francis up. The children were already bursting forth when we arrived, as fresh and lively as if they were just out of bed rather than after a full day's work. Very charming, almost angelic, they looked; but I was struck by the appearance of a haggard young woman who emerged from the building staring straight before her with dilated eyes and muttering 'Bedlam! Bedlam! Bedlam!' over and over again. It has ever been a mystery to me how, in a nannyless world, young mothers preserve their reason. There was an eminent doctor once who wanted the vote withdrawn from them, on the grounds that they could not be within measuring distance of sanity. Francis himself was a master of innocent but provoking mischief. That same morning his mother had found her cheque-book industriously completed in favour of herself and his father, schoolfriends, teachers, the milkman, no one forgotten. When the enormity of a deed was explained to him, he never repeated it, but he was endlessly fertile in new ideas. Whether he was typical or in a class of his own, I cannot say; but the memory of that young woman and her horror-filled eyes stayed with me long, indeed I can see her now.

Since he had been at this school, there were striking changes in his speech. The accent he had picked up was not Hereford at all but that indeterminate patois that used to be bluntly called 'common' and now is so often heard on the BBC that it might perhaps rate as Standard (II). Both of his parents spoke beautifully so that it must have been a trial, but they bore it patiently, reckoning that his prep school would deal with it by and by. And he would not have to feel out of things, as probably all the other new boys would be in the same boat.

From early days he showed himself a man of his time, with a quick, one might almost say innate, grasp of technical matters that were beyond me forever. He was quite at home with computers, for instance, and I am sure could have worked one if he got the chance. His taste in music was contemporary as well. His father Robin was reconstructing a roomy old barn some little way from the house or himself to retire to when Francis wanted to listen to Pop. This was necessary, he explained, if he was not to go berserk. Here again he showed his breadth of mind, for he loved good music and knew a great deal about it, and could hardly have been blamed if he had excluded that barbarous shindy from his dwelling altogether. There was nothing of the barbarian in Francis otherwise, however: he was a very urbane creature, a charming companion on a walk and never a bore.

Robin was a kind of eighteenth-century man, with a lively interest in everything and consequently an encyclopaedic knowledge. He also possessed a descriptive power which somehow raised everyday matters above their prosaic level and lent them a fairytale quality. For instance, their water supply came from Wales and was administered with a fair amount of skulduggery, but when Robin spoke of this it never seemed a question of Water Boards and civil servants but of malignant trolls damming and diverting their underground streams with evil intent against the human race. Penny had an Empire-building background and experience of natives in different parts of the globe and took it all in her stride with perfect equanimity.

It was a pleasure just to be with them and watch how they went to work. In their nonchalant way they were restoring the farmhouse to itself, not creating a sophisticated townsman's version of it, which happens all too often in the countryside at present. And there was a blessed peace in staying here, no neighbours in for drinks, no planned activities to amuse the guest, their normal life was refreshing and entertaining enough. Robin's mother, a brilliant woman, felt that he was burying himself and throwing his talents away, but I could never agree and it led to some very brisk discussion. But her attitude was rather complex, for at one moment she would declare that he was barking mad and in the next, angrily complain that he wasn't Prime Minister. I only wished that, if mad he was, there could be more madmen like him and, after all, it doesn't take much to be Prime Minister in Britain now.

Chapter Nine

The weekend at this delectable farm went all too swiftly by and Penny drove me to Hereford. On the way we came to Trumpet Cross, where our minor road ran across a main one, on a corner of which stood the Trumpet Inn. It must have been one of the most hazardous positions in England for such a place, for cars fairly scorch along the highway and its door opens directly on to it. Two convivial women met their end some time ago walking out of the bar and straight under the wheels of a lorry. They had fifteen children between them and never a husband: a local fund was set up and generously supported.

My one experience of Hereford was many long years ago but of poignant memory still. The BBC had misguidedly asked me to join a programme in the Town Hall there, when a panel of speakers would face a local audience and rap out answers to any questions put to them; and I, equally misguided, had agreed. Things might not have been so bad if the panel had consisted of those originally intended, all known to me personally or by name, but not one of them was there. We were a motley crew with nothing in common, the leading spirit (who should have been Stephen Potter) a cheery radio parson, a specialist in stating the obvious as if it had just come through to him by divine revelation. We were hardly on the air before my brain grew numb and in no time at all came the coup de grâce. Indiscipline in the schools was the theme, about which most of us had little to say, being neither parents nor teachers, and it fell to the Canon to straighten things out. Waving his pipe, he declared: 'The trouble is not with the schools or the children. The trouble – you're not going to like this, but I'll give it you straight from the shoulder – the trouble lies in THE HOME!' Rapturous applause followed these words, and he sat back beaming; but I was out for the count.

It did not seem fair that I should be paid for that protracted silence, and I subsequently returned the BBC's cheque; but they sent it back, as apparently the confusion in their books would have been, like myself, more trouble than it was worth. But they never asked me again, and I had forgotten the whole ignominious affair until the sight of Hereford Town Hall, so harmless and peaceful, brought it vividly to mind.

In Hereford now I had another of those pieces of accidental good fortune. Like so many of our ancient country towns, it is not the place for cruising about while you look for an hotel. The narrow streets are chockful of vehicles of every kind, and to park if only briefly is all but impossible. Penny therefore dropped me at the tourist office where, having a bulky case to drag along, I asked for the nearest accommodation. That turned out to be the Booth Hall, once a prison, then an asylum and now an inn, very clean and full of character, the service casual but pleasant and the food no worse than was to be expected.

The dining room was like the Common room of a college, with a raised platform at one end, a high vaulted ceiling with carvings, a carved stairway leading up to a gallery and coats of arms above the broad oldfashioned fireplace. One could imagine the big wigs of former times feasting and making merry here in Dickensian fashion while the prisoners beyond rattled their chains or the lunatics mopped and mowed. The present occupants were a group of happy young people sitting at a bar in one corner, dressed in their uniforms of T-shirt and exiguous jeans, with that familiar smile of bare flesh between the two.

More of the same were in the sunny garden outside, seated at large rustic tables and drinking prodigious amounts of beer without apparent discomfort, male and female alike. Each boy was paired with a girl, and two things about them were interesting, first, that as many girls were plain as pretty, as if the boys had chosen them for their qualities rather than as objects of admiration and envy to others, and second, that neither sex had made any effort to smarten itself up for the other. Where once the boys would at least have put on a clean shirt and combed their hair, and the girls would have got themselves up as attractively as they could, now they were content to stay as they were, grubby, unkempt, in garments frayed or torn. They were extremely pleasant, welcoming me with a delightful unconsciousness of our difference in age, which seems typical of the young these days; typically, too, they demanded my Christian name and used it, introducing themselves by their own and nothing more. Conversation between themselves consisted chiefly of badinage, a friendly non-stop teasing common to all ages in the English working-class which seems unable to express affection otherwise than by laughing at the object of it. Some were school-leavers and many had no job, but all for the moment were leaving the morrow to take care of itself. There appeared to be no lack of money and the girls all paid their way, fair and square.

After lunch I set out to explore, beginning with the Cathedral of St Mary the Virgin and St Ethelbert the King. From without it was looking benignly splendid this afternoon, with its beautifully kept Close, the bright spring green of its lawn, a smoky-blue wistaria tumbling down the front of one house and a tall chestnut in full white flower near the west door. Inside, however, there was a horrid surprise. It quite seemed as if a fair were being held in this holy place. Wooden frames had been set up to carry slogans of the Farmers' Union, posters on how to make cider and telling its history, photographs and garish cartoons glorifying British beef, bacon and vegetables. Then there were exhibits, a small, up-to-date and expensive tractor, various rubber articles, a spiked contraption on which you could fix your cotton spools and see at a glance the colour you wanted and, of course, a table displaying bottles and casks of cider and perry, all from firms roundabout. Boost for Hereford, in fact. A lady verger in a blue robe was handing out leaflets, from which I learned that this had been put together for Rogation Sunday, when 'the Church prays for God's blessing on the labour of men and on the fruits of the earth'. But surely there was no need to go about it in quite such a vulgar way. The Harvest Festival is a lovely one, with the churches a mass of flowers and all the good things, the fruit, vegetables, eggs, loaves, arranged in thankfulness before the altar; but this was cheap and nasty, as if an advertising agency had been given the job of mounting it.

I hoped that Evensong would take away the taste of this, but the Second Lesson was read from the New English Bible. Why, when the Authorized Version is one of the noblest and most beautiful books in our language, part of the inheritance of each one of us no matter what our religious affiliations may be, or if we have none, the Anglicans should inflict this flat commonplace rendering on their hapless church passes all understanding. There seems to be a notion abroad that everything must be tinkered with, brought up to date and into line with 'the needs of the people'; but the people were never consulted and, in fact, have never needed beauty and style more than today. How crude and insipid that Lesson did sound, compared to what it had replaced! But the choir was first-rate, the boys looking delightful in their blue gowns and white surplices with an Elizabethan ruff round their necks, and the lights in the choirstalls lit the young faces up from below with most charming effect. This choir joins with those of Gloucester and Hereford in the annual Three Choirs Festival, now one of the major events of the musical year, held turn and turn about in the three Cathedrals and thronged with people from everywhere.

As soon as the choir had gravely filed out, work was resumed on the exhibition, late arrivals having to be installed amid banging and scraping, and I put off further exploration until the following day. The Cathedral has so many treasures that one could spend whole weeks in examining them. The greatest of them perhaps is the Mappa Mundi, made by Richard de Bello and probably finished about 1300. It is the largest work of its kind in existence, one larger still in Germany having been destroyed in the war, but measures only 65 by 54 inches and the detail is not always easy to make out. Richard did not sign it but left a written prayer that those who heard of it or saw it should pray for his happiness in heaven.

Where, asks Prebendary A. L. Moir in a brief guide, did the author get his information? Where, indeed? For it is of a curious kind. The earth is pictured as flat, with Jerusalem at the centre, the map purporting to show the history of the

Christian faith as well as the features of the discovered world. So Palestine is greatly enlarged, Asia, Africa and Europe are compressed and distorted as in the mirror of a fun fair and the British Isles are unrecognizable, squeezed into the bottom lefthand corner. But the Sphinx is shown in Egypt, and so are the Pyramids: India rises to an elephant of sorts; and to the left of Asia is the Ark, with animals, on Mount Ararat. Encircling the earth is an impassable ocean; anyone who attempted to cross it fell into a bottomless pit.

Geography, scenes from the Old and New Testaments and natural history, however, are not the chief concern of this useful work. Four large letters, M O R S, are attached at equal distances to the periphery to remind us that death rules the world. Above it Christ in glory, surrounded by angels, is holding the Day of Judgement. Angels crown the kneeling Mary, summon the righteous to leave their graves and hand over the wicked to a fiend, who drags them off to be devoured by monsters.

Bello's main source was the Bible, but he also used the works of early Christian writers, pagan philosophers, classical authors, Roman army maps, myths, legends and travellers' tales, and drew freely on the bestiaries, the old monastic books with grotesque illustrations of bird and beast. It is strange to think of the monks in their cells drawing these mad figures out of their holy minds, basing them on what the not-so-holy travellers had recounted, giants, monsters, horned dogs, a one-legged man keeping the sun off his head with his one large foot ... They are every bit as wild as Herodotus, and he at least passed the weirder stories on for what they were worth, while the monks appear to have been in earnest. And as for Bello himself, the amount of study and erudition he poured into what today seems like an elaborate joke is positively awe-inspiring.

Then there is the chained library, with rows of ancient vellum books between stout leather covers, each one firmly chained to its shelf, a practice that other libraries might adopt in these degenerate days. It also has a fine collection of illuminated gospels and missals, including the Cider Bible, in Wycliffe's translation of about 1420, in which the word 'sidir' is used instead of 'strong drink' and a magnificent Gospel on which the bishops of Hereford still take their oath of installation. The library is reached by a climb of fifty-four steps, winding upwards in a turret too narrow for people to pass, so that once started you have to go on, and briskly too, not to annoy those behind. Happily, these are of solid stone, not open ironwork as in so many continental cathedrals where you become increasingly loth to look down and even fear to get stuck at the top, like a tree'd cat. This morning the entrance to these stairs was still shut half an hour after it was due to open. Spain has broken my spirit in such matters, and the other English, too, all waited quiet as sheep, but a fuming American asked a verger the reason for it and got the reply: 'The person in charge hasn't turned up. It's all voluntary, you see.' The American did not see and cut up so rough that the verger ran for one of the clergy, and thus we all got in.

The tombs are fascinating with their effigies, knights in armour with the snake-headed dogs lying at their feet, pious ladies, worldly clerics. One of these is Robert de Merlan, bishop of Hereford 1163–67, lying in a row of three others. He was a great theologian and a close friend of Thomas à Becket, but took the king's side in the quarrel and now rests here with the unlined face of those who judiciously seek their own interest. Another was of a married couple, the woman an heiress of seventeen having died in childbirth, her swaddled baby close at hand with a chrisom showing that it had been baptized before death, hastily perhaps by the midwife. Although the husband was buried there too, he had in fact survived her and married another rich girl elsewhere first.

But our cathedrals are the repository of more than ancient monuments and trophies, they preserve the decencies of former times and show through their clergy and staff an old-fashioned courtesy and patience. Of the latter, they probably had need, to judge from the young proles as they tramped about laughing and talking as if they were in a pub, indeed for all the world like those youngsters I had met at Booth Hall. Perhaps they were vaguely conscious of being out of their depth and hiding their uneasiness, English style, under a flow of facetious comment, or perhaps they looked upon the place as a showpiece or museum, a curious antique with life of its own and no relevance to theirs. And there were

90

even at this early season hordes of Germans, conversing in a kind of Wagnerian roar; but that was most likely their normal pitch and not intended as provocation. Most clearly of all I remember an immense child in a pushcart propelled by her mother, deep in conversation with a friend, staring ahead with blank blue eyes while it inflated its massive cheeks to puff out a bladder of pink bubble gum, sucking it in again to repeat the process over and over, unwearied. I could almost feel the shade of Kilvert at my elbow and hear his biting remarks, and suddenly it came to mind how someone not perhaps unlike him had pounced on me in Christ Church, Oxford, years ago, directing me to cover my head at once or leave: a sight such as this, I reflected, must have carried that poor man off altogether.

Between them all, they put the spirits of the temple to flight. I was chilled in any case by hours of wandering among slabs of stone and was glad to get into the warm light of day. In the pedestrians' centre I sat down on one of the benches and prepared to watch the citizens going about their occasions. Motorfree precincts are a happy innovation, sanctuaries from the roar and stench of traffic. Let us hope that they will spread over wider and wider areas, just as there are more and more places where one can dodge the fumes of tobacco. That of Hereford was particularly enjoyable, with its banks of flowers and throngs of cheerful attractive people, and it was good to hear the slow rumble of their country talk.

Nevertheless, I had reckoned without a new development in English life, one to be deplored: namely, the habit that strangers now have of falling into conversation at the drop of a hat. It is nothing short of revolutionary. In former times, a decorous dumbness was the rule, to be broken only in time of war or at Christmas. You might queue for an hour or sit all afternoon on a communal seat in the park without anyone saying a word. In the train you had only to open a newspaper to become instantly *incomunicado*, if not invisible; people were carried for miles out of their way rather than ask if this were their train until the Inspector came round. Only first-class commuters, having seen the same faces every working day for years, might venture on a quiet Good morning! before they sat down: hoi polloi in the third never uttered at all except if trodden on, when they would mutter 'pardon me'.

All this seems to have gone. One never is safe. Now an oldish man beside me burst into a flood of talk about the younger females who passed. He was a severe critic, moreover. Nearly everyone had something wrong, bandy legs, unbrushed hair, too much make-up, unsuitable clothes, and anything like embonpoint moved him to lively indignation. 'Look at Fatty!' he would growl as a Junoesque figure swept by. 'Wearing trousers, too!' His own proportions were ample, his belly cried out for a maternity smock, but he was either unaware of this or indifferent to it. And in common with this whole breed of compulsive chatterers, he took the interest of what he had to say for granted. In the past I have often known foreigners to be critical of our traditional reserve, putting it down to aloofness or pride. I think it was rather due to modesty and good manners, but whatever the cause, it was agreeable.

My garrulous neighbour being in full spate, I sneaked off to an empty bench some distance away.

Now a roar of 'Ted!' just behind it made me jump. A sturdy yokel had caught sight of a friend on the opposite side, and the pair fell into a real countryman's talk, bellowing at each other rather than cross the few yards between them. This could go on indefinitely, because male rustics can never quietly take their leave when they have had their say. An invisible lien holds them together until either one severs it at last by the delivery of a punch line; when he has done so, he turns abruptly on his heel and walks away, while his companion shouts with laughter. And so it fell out here, just as my eardrums were about to burst.

'Haven't seen Joe this whoile, Ted.'

'Nor you won't. His eyes be terrible bad again. Came up to the car one day just as I was startin' 'er and stood there a-chattin' and a-peering through the window like. "What's in the sack then, Ted?" says he, he was always a nosey bugger. "That's no sack, mate," says I.' A brief dramatic pause at this point. ' "THAT'S THE DEAR WOMAN!" '

And with these words he marched briskly off, while the other half of the act doubled up.

92

As I sat there, savouring the peace, a woman with two bulging carrier bags sat down beside me and burst into loud lamentation over the price of everything. Prices are fast superseding the weather as the cardinal topic of conversation, another change for the worse. You never know what the weather might do, and this left room for the surmise and speculation which made the subject, in capable hands, so rivetting. Prices on the other hand are sure to go steadily up and up. This woman too was clearly intending to run over her purchases, item by item, comparing figures with those of last month in the apparent belief that nobody else ever went shopping.

The pleasures of silent contemplation were seemingly not to be had in this matey forum, and I crept off, mourning again for the lost national reticence. I found further proof of that loss in the church of St Peter's nearby, where a board was covered with requests for prayers on all kinds of personal and intimate matters: for a little niece with a 'hearing problem', for a couple whose marriage was breaking up, for a youth who had failed an examination, for an invalid woman whose canary had died ... It must all be bound up with the open compassionate caring society, like Christian names at first sight, 'togetherness' and the Billy Butlin ethic in general.

Hereford is another delightful town in which to wander about with no particular aim, simply to enjoy the narrow crooked streets with their ancient houses and the homely oldfashioned stores and shops. The market did one's heart good, with its stalls of honest food, baskets of fresh brown eggs instead of pallid ones laid by tortured battery hens and stuck in a plastic container, well-baked crusty loaves instead of the limp and boiled, appetising vegetables that smelled of the earth, meat that had never been frozen, home-made jams with labels written in ink, all deliciously far away from the Instant Muck of the superstores. The shoppers looked like real housewives, too, choosing with care, the sort that would take pains with the cooking rather than dish up some ready-made prepacked concoction that defied analysis. I remembered a bizarre little exchange I had had in the Gloucester Road, where a supermarket for once was offering garden peas in their pods. An assistant whom I asked for a couple of pounds assured me that peas only came in boxes, small or large, and she could not say what they weighed.

'I don't want frozen peas, I want these fresh ones here,' I told her, indicating the pile.

'That's not peas,' she replied with scorn. 'That's vedge.'

She doubtless imagined that peas and beans grew in boxes, like boeuf stroganoff and apple-pie, and would have been greatly mystified among the exotic colours, shapes and scents of Hereford market.

That evening I could have wished one of the Hereford housewives had asked me to dinner, for I was rash enough to visit a restaurant written up in a local magazine. The puff was in the usual vein of those gastronomes who munch around and then delude the public with a description of their experience: 'We then sampled an exquisite home-made pâté, followed by a memorable roast duckling with etceteras and a creamy lemon meringue. The wine list here is somewhat restricted, but *bien soigné* . . . ', or words to that effect. What I got was the familiar American-style dog's dinner, frozen chicken cooked to a frazzle, a square inch of tasteless stuffing, a horny rasher of bacon and sodden chips all jumbled up in a lake of bisto gravy, with a few pigs of grapefruit on a lettuce leaf and a carafe of what seemed to be vinegar. A meal, in short, that was probably appearing on similarly candle-lit tables all over provincial England, and being eaten with equal gusto by a similar clientele, dressed up to the nines and coming it the gourmet with the waiter.

I read the paper, to take my mind off the victuals, and came on a story which seemed apropos. A Frenchman was brought to a police-station in Somerset after driving merrily along the right-hand side of the road and slap into an articulated lorry. Asked to explain this action, he confessed to having dined very well, remarkably well, at an inn where the food and wine were both excellent. 'Ah, I see what's happened,' the Sergeant said humanely, 'you must have thought you were back in France.' And the case was not pursued.

On my return, the decorous and peaceful Booth Hall was transformed, this being Saturday night and given up to contemporary folk culture. Dozens of teenagers were milling about the bars, while an infernal device ground out a selection of pop or punk or rock, or whatever it was, howls of what seemed to be agony alternating with shouts of apparent rage, accompanied by the merciless twang of electric guitars and the thud thud thud of some other instrument that I could not place. Now and then I caught a few words of a song, or imagined I did, for it hardly seemed possible that human beings could really be uttering them.

The youngsters, flushed and starry-eyed with beer, were greatly enjoying themselves and conversing in voices that easily rode above the din. They made room for me at the bar in the friendliest fashion, begging me to stay and share these singular pleasures; but I cut and ran as soon as I decently could.

Chapter Ten

From Hereford I was going on to stay with two new friends at Malvern. One was June, the daughter of Arthur Grimble, whose book *A Pattern of Islands* describing his experiences as Colonial Governor in the South Seas I had immensely enjoyed, and the other, Margaret, the teacher of Classics in the College for Girls. I had already spent a night or two with them as June had issued warm-hearted invitations through Sister Marian at Stanbrook with a note of 'My house is yours, burn it' about them before ever setting eyes on me.

That connection I had found somewhat puzzling at first, for the two of them seemed to have nothing whatever in common; but I soon discovered one link at least. Both were cat worshippers, as Margaret also was, and this curious passion played an important part in the lives of all three. I am a dog lover myself, a very crude down-to-earth article compared with the devotees of the cat. Much as I appreciate a dog's delightful qualities I cannot possibly tell you what is passing in his mind at any given moment of the day, basing my analysis on a twitch of a whisker or similar evidence; and if he leaves his food untasted I assume that he is not hungry, without tormenting myself over the spiritual reasons which may lie behind this. Moreover, I suspect that cats are the most finished and perfect of humbugs and while they pose as mysterious, aloof and fastidious are merely playing hard-to-get.

That is by the way, however, and I was greatly looking forward to the visit and to exploring Malvern, a town as different from either Worcester or Hereford as anything so short a distance away could be.

It is, in some respects, a town of strange contradictions. It is full of nursing-homes and schools, is bourgeois to the core and obviously well-conducted, and yet you may often see there that unusual sight in these days, a bobby on his beat, as well as which numbers of police-cars are on patrol, as if struggling with a crime wave. It is built on the side of a hill, many of the slopes rising so abruptly that to climb them is a penance; and yet the place has an irresistible appeal for the elderly and infirm. Wherever you are, there are people with white hair, bent backs and shaky limbs toiling upward and onward. Spaniards apparently make a point of choosing the most awkward site available for their towns and villages: Madrid is the supreme example, with nothing to recommend it whatsoever; but the English as a rule pay attention to convenience and comfort. Not so the founding fathers of Malvern.

Then, the amount and range of intellectual and cultural activity is stupendous, to judge from the notice-board in the Public Library. Meetings of learned bodies and societies, talks on travel, poetry, drama, food, the wisdom of the East and, of course, gardening, country rambles under expert leadership, archaeological digs, amateur music-making and madrigal singing – I have never seen such a plethora before. Yet the inhabitants look neither arty nor brainy. They are, by and large, comfortable tweedy old dears, much taken up with their dogs, who often bear a mysterious facial resemblance to them; and they have, even by English country-town standards, a notable sweetness of manner.

The pace of life is practically oriental. To collect money from the Bank, change your library books and visit a few shops will run away with the morning. Few are so vulgar as simply to get what they want and be gone. They must always have a chat with the people who serve them, so cosy and gentle, so unaware of anyone fidgeting in the queue behind. When they chance to meet someone they know, they settle down to a real confabulation, right in the middle of the pavement, and everyone must step off it in order to pass them.

I happened to come on such a pair of women just as one was plaintively remarking to the other, 'So *unnecessary*, and a great mistake.' It took me back to my youth, when my elders reserved this particular judgement for the gravest of matters, from a Royal abdication down. It was once applied, I remember, to the heir of a noble house on his turning Catholic; and now, like the speaker herself with her rose-petal complexion and modulated tones (for a lady never raises her voice) it seemed to conjure up a bygone age.

Feigning interest in the nearby shop, I paused to find out what had called it forth.

'Exactly my own feeling,' replied the second: *quite unnecessary.*'

'What can the BBC be thinking of? I am surprised they put such a programme out.'

It sounded like the soft cooing of doves.

'They don't much mind what they say these days.'

'If there is no hereafter, no resurrection, what is the point of all this?' continued the first lady, with a restrained gesture towards the busy street, the passersby and the gourmet foods in Everton's window.

'Precisely. It should never have been allowed.'

'And so soon after Easter, too. I thought it in very poor taste.'

'Perhaps we should write to the Governors?'

'I have already done so.'

They were clearly the salt of the earth, a thought which reminded me that I had to get a drum of Essex salt that morning, and I went into Everton's to do this. When I came out, after the ritual Malvern delays, there they were, still quietly deploring the laxity of the BBC and contemporary trends altogether. It seemingly never occurred to them to switch a programme off and forget it: no, their duty as Englishwomen was to hear things out to the bitter end and then take some one or other mildly to task.

I was on my way just then to the great Priory church, which stands about halfway up this thoroughfare of shops with everything for middle-class comfort. It is a splendid building in late Perpendicular, originally begun soon after the Conquest, with additions in the thirteenth and four-teenth centuries, including a Lady Chapel that was des-troyed after the dissolution of the monasteries. The outer walls are charmingly coloured, some of a sand-yellow, others, rosy pink, and with the sun on them the contrast to the vivid green of the grass, the sombre grey slabs of granite marking ancient tombs and the dark-leaved trees overhead is enchanting.

The Priory is famous for its fifteenth-century stained glass, second only to that of York Minster, much buffeted by time and weather but still magnificent. The chief treasure is the north transept window, showing in different scenes the Joys of Mary, the Virgin herself dominating the whole, standing on high within a broad circle of heavenly blue, the deep blue of a sapphire. The pictures are small and somewhat crowded, so that the detail is hard to make out, but all the colour is rich and pure as that of a jewel, ruby, amethyst, emerald or topaz, and when the sun shines through it the window seems ablaze. We can imagine the beauty of this interior when the original glass was still intact.

In one of the guides, by the way, this window is named The Coronation of Mary, which may be due to an unfortunate mix-up: for a few windows away to the west there is an insipid nineteenth-century Coronation of Queen Victoria. There are three lower panels, the lefthand one showing the dear Queen as a girl, receiving news of her accession – 'I *will* be good' – giving rise perhaps to thoughts of the Annunciation. In the centre, the Crown is being placed on her dutiful head; and on the right, she is at prayer, with the Prince Consort near by. Above is the figure of Our Lord, flanked by kneeling blacks and browns who raise their hands to Him in thankfulness for her rule. I only raise the possibility of some misapprehension, as the crowd in front of this is often considerably larger than that before the masterpiece itself.

On the noticeboard in the grounds today there was the announcement of a Jazz Cantata, called 'Captain Noah and his Floating Zoo', to be performed on the following Sunday. The players were all from the congregation, one of them a retired percussionist who had travelled for years with Mantovani's dance band, and I made a careful note of the time in order not to be present. It must be ruefully admitted that trendiness has rather taken hold of the place these days. All kinds of activities go on which are hardly in keeping with its grave and holy spirit, concerts of secular music, for example, at which one is urged to 'feel free' to clap, something I will never get used to. In England, that is to say, for the boisterous row that goes on when the Pope is carried into St Peter's has something agreeably child-like about it; but one has some little idea that the English are adult people and ought to restrain themselves.

In the porch were the Four Clappers of the Old Ring, mounted on a wooden back with a verse inscribed:

> Our duty done in Belfry high,
> Now voiceless tongues at rest we lie.

and presented by Edward Archer. They brought to mind the peal of English bells on Sunday morning, clear and merry yet soft, so different from the racket abroad, as of a poker banging upon a pail. Our foundries must have had a special way of treating the metal, for I never heard a foreign chime to compare with ours – as they used to be, that is. Bellringing seems to be on the way out with so much else that is precious; I have even heard horrible canned muzak-type records being broadcast over a loud-speaker, to which complete, utter silence would be infinitely preferable.

This morning a week-day Communion service was being held, with a feminine congregation of different ages but one social class, namely, the upper-middle. Can there be another religious body in the world so entirely homogeneous? No one says, Proles Keep Out, they simply do. The Church of England has been described as the Tory party at prayer, but these mild-eyed ladies had nothing of Tory fire about them: they seemed to inhabit a world in which reality was kept at arm's length, a Winnie-the-Pooh and Wind-in-the-Willows world, along with tennis parties and cucumber sandwiches, gardening and bridge, cats and dogs. The parson was intoning a hideous new liturgy in the faultless accent which has begun to sound like an affectation. I amused myself imagining the scene were some latter-day Savonarola to burst in with vehement warnings of hellfire and brimstone – 'Ignore him, dear, those people never know when to stop.' 'But so unnecessary . . .' – and wondered if all this urbanity arose from the fact that no one really believed any longer.

But a polite little notice begged visitors not to walk about during a service, and I went away to continue exploring the

100

town itself. The architecture is mostly deplorable, Victorian Gothic, or aiming to look Baronial, or merely nondescript; but the houses will be set as a rule in a beautiful garden, the plants chosen and placed with a discerning eye for colour and design. How can people who are capable of producing the second even tolerate the first? And how can those who revel in ugly building have so fine a sense for natural beauty? The best point from which to get a general view is about three quarters of the way up the hill, so that you have the peak still above you and the wide sweep of the vale below. Then the individual houses are mercifully screened by trees, with only steeples and spires rising through, which gives a misleadingly romantic air to the whole panorama.

Preparations now were going ahead for the Festival, a somewhat mixed affair to please all tastes, from Eliot and Shaw at the theatre to Rock-n-Roll in the Nag's Head. This redoubtable tavern had already made a deep impression on me, by having a specially vile fruit machine which made belching and vomiting noises when somebody won a prize. An old-fashioned fair was being set up on the Common, there was a barbecue promised, and a Fringe Pub-Crawl, described as an 'intellectual inquiry into the appreciation of various local hostelries'. Hardly less daunting was 'A Festival Aperitif of Prose, Poems and Music by the Malvern Writers' Circle', offered on the very first day. There were also recitals galore, in which a more than ample justice would be done to the local great man, Elgar. Moonshine – an evening of constructive rock, at the Nag's Head again. Plainly, there was to be never a dull moment.

Flags were flying, bunting was rife about the streets, the top cashier in the Bank wore a red carnation in his buttonhole, but there was nothing festive in the air, no continental gaiety, not even of the dogged German sort. The English are probably incapable of it. To begin with, they do not really approve of festivals, or anyhow not of the kind of person who gets them up, nor do they care for foreigners, whom they see as a visitation or cross, to be calmly and politely borne but not to put oneself out for. And foreigners were pouring in by the hundred now, losing their way and getting in everyone else's, looking woebegone as cats under the ruthless rain.

101

Some resistance there was, reflected in the *Malvern Gazette*, an organ powerfully combined with the *Ledbury Reporter*. The Malvern Hills Conservators, I read, were greatly vexed by the fair, which in previous years had damaged the ground and left piles of rubbish about, and also by the owner's cavalier treatment of their complaints. One of them now demanded that he be banned from the Common, while he in turn threatened in that case to black it to all other fairs through the Showman's Guild. Also, the noise of roundabouts and fruit machines upset the genteel inhabitants of Graham Road near by, especially those in the old folks' home on the corner, a handsome dwelling in spacious grounds, built by Perrins, the creator of Worcestershire Sauce. Incidentally, the firm of Perrins, after 150 years of dedicated service to Man, had suddenly gone on strike, seeking parity with the makers of tomato ketchup. These and other items of general interest, the threats and counter-threats all made for lively reading, as local papers invariably do. I went to call on the editor but unhappily he was in Worcester, putting the next issue to bed.

Next day, the affair was to open with the carnival. Fortunately the rain had stopped, the sun came out, the bedraggled flowering shrubs pulled themselves together and Malvern wore a beaming smile. In the Winter Garden the noble Davidia or Handkerchief tree had marked the occasion by bursting into bloom, a mass of two-lipped flowers, white with a centre button of scarlet, tumbling through the bright green leaves and smelling deliciously of lime. The Carnival was to wend its way up the long road from the Link to Great Malvern, and spectators were already lining the route when we got there. Presently the *cortège* of floats and banners was seen to be moving in our direction, headed by a brass band played by Brownies, Cubs and a Guide or two with notable competence. A deal of thought and patient effort had gone into the making of the floats, but our national decorum inhibited those who manned them from displaying anything like brio. The ones in fancy dress had a particularly hangdog air, like mutes at a funeral. An exception to this was a group of old ladies sitting in the back of an open lorry which had been got up to look like a garden. I cannot say if their flowing dresses and large flowery hats were intended as period pieces or were simply their habitual wear, but they were very much at their ease and apparently unconscious of everything round them. Each had an open upturned parasol on the ground beside her, and the public were expected to shy coins into them in aid of a local charity. I did so with a will, but lost confidence after scoring a direct hit on a lady's hat, while she continued to gaze serenely ahead with eyes that took nothing in. Another exception were a few of the clowns who had thoughtfully come provided with masks: secure in their face-lessness, they could afford to spread themselves a little.

I had half imagined that bears would figure in the proceedings somehow, as the cult of them appeared to be gathering momentum all over the land. The latest manifestation was at Longleat, where Lord Bath had assembled the biggest collection of stuffed Bruins the world had ever seen. Two live cuddlies from Canada, resident on the place, were to act as compères to the show, and it was whispered that the famous Miss Barbara Cartland might look in after opening the Honey Fair, if, the *Observer* said, 'she got the bees out of her bonnet sufficiently.' There would be other celebrities too, and marmalade sandwiches, and gingerbread bears, as well as the odd fleeting glimpse of the Marquess. I must confess that, were I an English grandee, I would sell out and live in a council house or converted barge before polluting the ancestral home in this way.

In the event, the Carnival produced nothing ursiform, live, stuffed or Teddy, which seemed an opportunity missed.

When the procession had gone its decorous way, I strolled down towards the Common. The Reverend Walters was sitting on his favourite bench and looking across the huddled swings, roundabouts and stalls of the fair to the lovely prospect beyond. He had been a housemaster at Uppingham and now lived in the house where I was staying, which was divided into three. His wife and he were both much liked by my hostesses, both in their different ways being excellent company. Mrs Walters was a decided character who never shrank from positive statements, whatever the subject might be. Only the other day she had declared as a fact that our grisly weather was due to Divine Indignation at Whitsuntide being supplanted by the pagan Spring Bank Holiday. The family theologian allowed the assertion to pass, no matter what his thoughts may have been; they were a most devoted couple and set each other off delightfully.

Now he proposed that we should walk down and have a look at the fair, about which there was great difference of opinion. Certainly, there was a fine volume of noise, as the merry-go-rounds, the fruit machines and the juke boxes all poured their separate offerings into the common fund. The ladies in the Perrins Home at the Common's edge might well object, accustomed as they were to low voices, gently opening and shutting doors and a cushioning of the nervous system altogether. And not only they, but the inmates of similar establishments further along, for the Graham Road is a kind of geriatric reservation: there seem to be snowy heads in almost every window, like those fluffy white balls on pine trees that a pest has spun. But the uproar only lasts a couple of weeks, after which their peace should seem doubly peaceful, while the children looked forward to their deafening treat for months ahead. Mr Walters stood it with fortitude and waited uncomplaining as I tried my luck with the bandits and tombolas; his experiences at Uppingham had possibly left him noise-proof.

There were a number of things I would have liked to ask him about his time at the school. The frightfulness of public schools is a perennial topic of English conversation, but always among the 'boys', aged anything up to seventy. Bullies galore, grisly food, living quarters similar to those of a Victorian gaol, merciless beating, from my own childhood on I have been reading or hearing about them. I remember Cyril Connolly almost in tears as he told of floggings at Eton, and the notion came to me that perhaps he was lucky not to have been garotted. Such intense self-pity and bitter recrimination years and years after the event were unattractive. But suffering, apparently, was not confined to delicate literary souls like his. Gerald Templar, as tough a nut as could be, used to point out a window in his old school house from which he had nearly thrown himself in his despair. Can it be that young males create a hell around them by some frightfulness of their own? I should have welcomed the views of Mr

Walters on this subject, but he was at his most urbane this evening and it might have struck a jarring note.

Instead I told him the story of an Irish builder who was commissioned to put up a protective wall round a national monument, a ruined chapel or such like. He made a nice neat job of the wall, but when it was finished the monument was nowhere to be seen, for he had innocently used the stones in the building. Mr Walters' delighted comment was, 'There have to be people like that in the world!' a kindly attitude that did him honour. My own opinion was that there should not be too many of them and that they were better to hear about than to deal with.

Before we parted, he tipped me off about a concert to be held in the Priory that same evening, given by the choir of St Michael's College, Tenbury. Somehow he always appeared to be supernaturally well informed about such doings, or perhaps he benefitted from a clerical grapevine denied to the rest of us. Certainly I had heard nothing of it, nor seen anything in the crowded hall of the Public Library, mirror of the vigorous cultural life of the town. The concert began as dusk was falling and the choir were a charming spectacle in their scarlet robes and white ruffs under the soft lamplight; and they sang most beautifully, beginning with delicious works by Purcell, Byrd and Arne, all received by the packed audience with rapturous applause. But after the interval they resumed with a piece from Brückner, which met with exactly the same fervid response, as if the hearers believed that one thing must be equal to another, provided it was Serious Music and performed in a Priory. I hastened out before the musicians carried out their plan of following this up with Vaughan Williams and the inevitable Elgar, whose motto appears to be 'anything Mahler can do, I can do worse'.

Shaw is another Old Man of the Sea in Malvern without the Elgar excuse of being either born or buried there, and is doggedly performed in season after season. It seems an odd choice for so mature a public, for one would have thought the combination of brilliant clown and pompous didact would be more attractive to the young. At sixteen I myself was mad about him. Now here he was again, with *Heart-*

105

break House and the only alternative was T. S. Eliot's *The Elder Statesman*, to which I accordingly went.

The theme was one which always seems to go down well with English audiences, namely, the follies of youth rising up to confound successful and respected age. While at university, the Statesman had encouraged a young friend in expensive tastes (probably he needed little encouragement or none) which led the boy to crime, prison and disgrace; and he had also seduced a chorus girl, which also perhaps had been no major task. The reappearance of the pair, smarting from their wrongs after all these years, gave rise to great heartsearching on the part of the hero, persuading him that his whole career was somehow invalidated. It could have been a delightful frolic, a highbrow version of that perennial favourite, the banana-skin situation, but alas it was overclouded by deep thoughts about purification through remorse. Oddly enough, it is only now, today, that I realize what had really gummed things up. A while ago some unknown benefactor sent me a copy of *Chicago Letter and Other Parodies* by W. B. Scott, in which there was a truly diabolical take-off of *The Cocktail Party*, and the mystery of Eliot, as a dramatist, was suddenly made clear: he wrote the plays as if he were parodying himself, and one was struck again and again by the deadly accuracy of his observation. Tonight's audience, however, a typically 'Eliot' one with their long, mild, earnest faces, obviously considered the occasion an intellectual treat.

Outside the theatre, afterwards, a curious little to-do seemed rather in the Eliot vein, a worried tourist lady having ordered a taxi which had not turned up and now appealing for sympathy to the crowd at large.

Lady: I made so sure the hotel got it right,
           Asking that they repeat both place and hour,
           Not once but several times.

Voice: There is so little service nowadays.
           You might say, almost none.

Lady: It is not as if I knew my way about.

2nd Voice: And have you far to go?

Lady: I'm none too certain of that, actually.
            The driver seemed to bring me in a flash.
            Yet, busy with my thoughts, I could have been
            Mistaken.

3rd Voice: My car is here. I should be very pleased
            To run you home. The important thing is,
            After all, that you should get there.

Lady: Indeed, but that is just the trouble.
            I quite forget the name of my hotel ...

No one could come to grief in caring compassionate Malvern, however, and we may rest assured that somehow a solution was found.

Chapter Eleven

Indeed Malvern struck me as the cosiest blandest town I had ever met, in even this 'land of such dear souls'. I remember reading of a hideous crime wave that was sweeping the area round-about, bicycles continually stolen in Ledbury, a boutique in Kidderminster broken into and the petty cash removed, cars borrowed in more places than one, a crate of beer seized off a lorry in Upton – an outside job this, it was thought, for no Uptonian would have done it – but of Malvern never a word. Margaret and June, loth as they were to concede that the town lagged behind in any respect, could point to nothing worse than the occasional upsetting of dustbins or the seizure of their lids. No doubt to look into the matter thoroughly I should have called on the local police and asked for their views: to hear, perhaps, 'Well, we've had no theft or breakings in, but a hitherto respected man has been convicted of riding his tricycle along a pavement in darkness, without a light.'

Only one little scene brought home to me in sudden vivid fashion that Malvern was part of contemporary England after all. I was waiting for a bus when a girl of fourteen or so, with fair curls and rosy face, came by pushing a pram. Older sister, I assumed, or kind young neighbour, taking Baby out while Mum got on with her housework. But then a bevy of other girls, in school tunics and straw boaters, ran up and surrounded the pram, full of admiration for its little incumbent; and from their remarks it was clear that this apparently helpful child was in fact the proud Mum. Their friendly interest and approval were delightful to see, as were the airs of their detrimental class-mate, who obviously plumed herself among other things on her premature escape from school. Somebody told me later that the offspring of such early beginners was apt to be especially bright and beautiful; let us hope that this is true.

The pleasant weather was keeping up, and my two hostesses often took me out into the countryside on a midday safari, lunching at this, that and the other pub. Just to sit in a car with this couple was as good as a play. Margaret was a compulsive map-reader and would sit with her nose buried in one while we flashed past trout streams, primrose, daffodil or bluebell woods, manor houses or cottages with their crowded fragrant little gardens, remarking from time to time that perhaps we should have turned left at the last crossroads or that now we should look out for the 'A'-something or other. My opinion was never asked because I cannot read a map, or rather I refuse to try. On the other hand, I always know where I am – you do or you don't, it's one of those things. June had no eye for country as such, only for the separate items in it, trees, animals, bridges, that she needed for a painting or a design; but she was an excellent driver and critical of poor performance, whether her own or other people's. It may have been the artistic temperament that made her every now and then do something outrageous; and when this happened and a vehement hooting broke out from the car behind she would comment, 'Quite right, quite right' with much approval.

I must record an occasion when she avoided a nasty accident, in fact probably saved our lives, by her skill and calm. We were going along a narrow winding lane with hedges so high and thick that there was no seeing or hearing what lay ahead when suddenly a youth hurtled round a bend towards us at motorway speed. You would have thought he had the world to himself. It happened so fast, there was hardly time to be frightened, and a head-on collision seemed inevitable; but June somehow managed to pull up and go into reverse in one move, accelerating meanwhile as one accelerates out of a skid, and we bowled smoothly backwards until the idiot boy had ground to a halt a yard or so from our bonnet. He then reversed as well, shooting backwards along the lane as fast as he could, grimly followed by us, until he came to an open gate-way into which he turned, pulling up and leaping out of the car. June slowed down, thinking that he wanted to apologize, but not a bit of it, he merely tore away on foot as if the Furies were after him without a glance in our direction.

'Gentleman driver!' was what we ought to have said, for the

109

least little error of judgement on the part of a woman invariably draws a growl of 'lady driver' from men. For a while June was pensive after that, and I feared she was belatedly suffering from nervous shock. In fact she was meditating on the boy with an artist's detachment, trying to find a possible explanation of his conduct. A romantic soul, she presently announced that he had been crossed in love and no longer cared what became of him. My view of the matter was that either the car was stolen and he on the run, or he was hoping to reach a pub before it shut. But I was too thankful to be in one piece to argue about it much.

That was the only disagreeable adventure we had, however, and our trips went off happily as a rule. The ideal way to make them would have been on horseback, sitting high enough to see over the hedges and across country and turning off the road at will to follow some woodland path or river bank. But apart from the hideous expense of hiring mounts today there was the question of time, as Margaret could never stay out of her classroom for long. We would drive out until we came to a pub that looked inviting, eat a hasty snack lunch and then wend our leisurely roundabout way back to her seat of learning in Malvern.

The pubs round here were as varied inside as their exteriors were uniformly attractive, and we never quite knew what lay in store for us. A sleepy little old house with mullioned windows, rose pond and goldfish pool, might turn out to be a hotbed of fruit machines and juke boxes. Another of equally deceptive appearance might be stuffed with every harlotry imaginable, from hunting horns or flights of plaster ducks against a wall to souvenirs of holidays abroad. Another might scorn the homely fare we wanted and offer scampi, chicken or whitebait 'in basket', an American dodge for charging more. This kind was apt to be full of elderly people, the ladies of a wonderful suburban chic with blue-rinsed hair, and it puzzled me where they could all have sprung from. Others were everything that we could wish for, plain, simple, friendly, used by farmers and horsey folk who knew each other, with no one trying to make an impression on anyone else.

There was one that we held in great esteem and affection.

It stood a little way from Ledbury on a country road, a solid farmhouse of rosy brick with stables and barns and an expanse of grass amounting almost to a private village green ringed by trees where you could sit and enjoy the view across a little valley as you drank. There was a slap-up restaurant that we did not visit, and a roomy wine and snack bar with furnishings that were mellowed by use and age rather than picked up in an antique shop. And there was something uncanny about it too, something literally attractive, because if we tried to find it we never could but when we cruised at random in the area Felicitas the car, sagacious vehicle, often brought us to it of her own accord.

One of the joys of this countryside was the number of animals everywhere, herds of cattle, flocks of sheep, mares running with their foals, all adding to the beauty of the scene. Perhaps the farmers had not heard, or did not wish to hear, of those satanic factories where creatures spend their lives in prison blocks until they are ready for slaughter, never feeling the sun and rain on their backs or grazing peacefully at will. It is odd, with the growing public concern for wild life in distant foreign parts, that there should be such indifference to the plight of animals here at home. And we lose by it as well, for a landscape without them is chilling and forlorn, as a wood or garden would be without its birds.

Pigs must have been specially singled out for this barbarous treatment, for they are seldom seen about these days. I am a fervent admirer of this intelligent and spirited animal, and never can understand how he got his bad name. He is not dirty at all, fastidious rather, if his sty is properly kept, and he is only gross because of the gross human taste for his fat, to produce which he is cooped up and stuffed like a Strasbourg goose. His guzzling is, as any psychiatrist will agree, but a compensation for the full rich life which his nature demands and man refuses. I had the care of some young pigs once during the war, and encouraged them to run and skip and leap from sty to sty: I had them lithe and taut as greyhounds until the farmer put a stop to it. And think of the pigs of Spain, those slim fast gingerhaired ones, getting their food for themselves under oak and fruit trees,

111

easily outstripping goats and sheep in their cross country runs! If there was ever a maligned species, pigs are it.

So then it was a pleasure to come on a farm one day devoted entirely to pigs and surrounding them with every comfort and convenience. We had lunched at a goodhearted pub called The Moon in Mordiford and were driving back through woodlands still in their delicious early green. At the foot of a steep hill there was a farm, with a few gigantic boars ambling about in the sunny courtyard, watched by a dog seated importantly on the roof of an outhouse. We stopped for a closer look, June having a pig project on hand at the moment, and a man called out to ask if we would like to come in and see the nursery. There were several lying-in sties full of beautifully clean straw, four of them taken up by litters of various sizes: one proud mother had brought forth seventeen, but she had only thirteen teats and some of the piglets were on the bottle. The sow lay on her side with her eyes shut, woofling and grumbling as if to say it was a nice thing how a woman never could have herself to herself but with a curly grin of satisfaction on her chops all the same. The star turn was a day-old lot, who were enchanting with their transparent ears, shell-pink bodies with a rose-coloured stripe down the backbone and their eager dark little eyes. There was a runt among them, half the size of the rest, but his position worried him not at all, as he climbed over the backs of his nuzzling brothers and sisters and pushed them off a teat when he fancied it for himself.

By chance that same evening as I looked through a volume of charcoal drawings by Henry Moore I found the study of a pig which seemed to give the very essence of his being, massive and languid in body but vigorous in mind, as shown by the alert ears, the furrowed brow, the sensitive snout and the wide flaring nostrils of a dreamer: all that I had vaguely thought and felt about him expressed in a few masterly lines.

In our expeditions the sight of so many creatures leading a happy natural life was a great pleasure indeed, but it was not the only one. There were the splendid trees, oak, elm and ash, dotted about in the meadows as if planted there deliberately with space on either side to spread as far as they liked. We were always coming on scenes that might have gone straight on to an artist's canvas without his needing to compose or rearrange: the background perhaps a long low hill with a wood like the hogged mane of a horse running along the top, the main feature some mighty oak of perfect form and round it a flock of sheep, grazing or lying down with such harmonious effect, they seemed to have thought it all out most carefully. We blessed the farmers who allowed those trees to stand and delight everyone who saw them, rather than cut them down like good businessmen for the sake of a little extra grass. Theirs was a welcome change from attitudes in some other regions, in East Anglia for example, and in truth there was a loving spirit about this countryside altogether.

These trips were necessarily confined to a small area because of Margaret's need to get back to her pupils, and yet there was a great variety in them, both of landscape and building. And I so thoroughly approved of her civilizing activities that I could not regret the shortness of them. To my consternation, however, one day she announced that she was expecting to go on a course of computer management. Asked to explain this rash and frivolous scheme, she said that it had been so decided because of modern conditions, with a probable falling away of interest in the classics and the need to look for alternatives. I was shocked to the core of my being, and referred her to Evelyn Waugh's opinion of such matters as set forth in his *Scott-King's Modern Europe*. She has read most things, but not this one; I told her that Scott-King had, in similar fashion, been asked to consider teaching other subjects, more likely to fit his boys for the modern world and quoted his imperishable reply: 'I should think it wicked to do anything which might fit a boy for the modern world.' She was struck by the force of it but in due course went off all the same.

My stay with them was as pleasant as could be. The Malvern cosiness had seeped into their interior like a gentle fog but there was nothing insipid about it, thanks to their lively intelligences. And the household was run with an efficiency which surprised me. From June, with her Government House background, one might have expected the peculiar slovenliness so often found in the post-Colonial class, which

113

I think must come from having been always, but very incompetently, waited on hand and foot, so that squalor, being irremediable, is a part of life; and from Margaret, the indifference to cleanliness and comfort that I have frequently observed in Oxford people of either sex. But not a bit of it: the place was kept in perfect order with a minimum of fuss and an outside helper only once a week.

The two of them made their guest feel entirely free and yet looked after, a hospitable art of which England has the secret. I relished it all, the books, music and pictures, the discussions of a sound reactionary nature, the boldly experimental meals and even the mild obsession with the cat.

'Is she in?'

'No. She is out. She has been out all day.'

'She hasn't touched her food.'

'Oh dear. What has upset her? That dog again?'

'Very likely. We shall have to do something about him.'

But it was not the dog, it was the presence of myself. Pussy was in a tantrum, partly because now and then I sat down on something she thought of as hers and partly because she no longer received undivided attention. She manifested her indignation by fasting, absenting herself for hours or leaving the room in a marked manner the instant I came in: it was the normal feline technique but it distressed her kindly owners and something had to be done. Seldom in my life have I worked so hard on personal relations as I did with that crafty brute and by the time I left she had come round, purring like a kettle whenever I stroked her ears. My friends warmly congratulated me, saying that she had never taken to an outsider before and that obviously I was a Cat Person after all: the discovery seemed to put the seal of success on my visit.

Chapter Twelve

Upton-on-Severn is a small town lying between Malvern and Tewkesbury which has the peaceful air of a village: looking at it today, it is strange to think of all it has endured from civil war and plague. It has a Courthouse of its own, a beautiful Queen Anne building, to give it status; and there are many reminders of when this river was one of the busiest waterways in Europe. All manner of craft tie up here yet, narrow boats or barges, cabin cruisers, yachts, houseboats and dinghies. The current flows along at a spanking pace, and a heavy rainfall or melting snow from the Malvern Hills can lead to flooding, accepted by the inhabitants with philosophy as a normal part of life.

Much has been done to improve drainage and create diversions, but in former times it could not so easily be shrugged off. For the men who used the bridge as a meeting place for gossip or to look for work the sight of corpses bobbing about in the water, whether of human beings or animals, was not uncommon. In the great flood of 1770, the worst for three centuries, scores of people were lost and infants in their cradles were seen drifting away across fields. In the parish records the entry 'Drowned in Severn' crops up time and again. The second biggest inundation occurred as late as 1852, when Upton became an island and even houses believed to be safe had muddy waves lapping their window-sills; and we are told that in this hour of trial the indomitable citizenry would row themselves to the bar of their favourite hotel.

Another hazard arose from the practice of dumping garbage, and worse, any old where that seemed handy. It led to a poisoned water supply and this, being cheerfully drunk or used in cooking, meant outbreaks of horrible disease. The cholera brought to England in 1832 by foreign seamen struck

115

hard here, meeting with every encouragement and carrying off as many as fifty people a month from a population of only 2000. A vivid account of their sufferings was given decades later by Emily Lawson, wife of the parson and the town's first chronicler, who collected the material from survivors. Friends and neighbours, however sympathetic, shunned the cottages where cholera victims lay and left them to die in agony. The corpses were buried in a piece of unconsecrated land called Parson's Field, half a mile from the town: one of the first was a woman by the name of Church and Mrs Lawson quotes the man who carted the body as saying 'Folk need not fret about there never being a Church in Parson's Field', for he had put one in himself – a grisly jest for which the Lord struck him down in turn, and his wife a few days later. Today this field is quite neglected, with only a plain inscription CHOLERA BURIAL GROUND 1832 on the low wall round it, a typical case of the stiff upper lip perhaps, when one thinks of the exuberant *Pest Säulen* in Austria, with their elaborate rococo carvings, put up in thanksgiving once the scourge had gone: or perhaps the difference of period explains it, for the plague in Austria was still a divine visitation and its passing a divine mercy, whereas the nineteenth-century Englishmen well knew that their own bad habits were largely to blame.

I first met Mrs Lawson through a contemporary Guide, which drew freely on her book *The Nation in the Parish* for many things of interest apart from the cholera. This guide, like that to Hanley Castle, was put together with loving care and close attention to detail: as, for instance, in the two illustrations of an identical street, the only difference being that in one of them a tree has had its branches lopped, a significant fact to which the reader's attention is carefully drawn. But the excerpts from Mrs Lawson were so lively and attractive that I went chasing after the book itself, now somewhat hard to find, and was well rewarded for my pains. Mrs Lawson was a natural writer, keenly observant, humorous, with a warm sympathy for Upton people of every class and a most un-Victorian lack of disapproval. Her few sharp words are kept for the oppressive or cruel, as we see from her description of the local ducking- (or goom- in Worcestershire) stool for scolds, a subject often treated with levity. 'The poor wretch was strapped into the chair at one end of a long beam, which was worked by a lever, so that she could be ducked into the water over and over again, while her tormentors stood on dry land.' The inhabitants of the nearby cottages 'must have had a good view of these scenes of riotous vengeance; perhaps their doors may have been opened to receive the wretched woman when she crawled away from her degrading punishment, half-drowned, and too much exhausted and terrified to reach her own home.' The practice was discontinued more than a hundred years before Mrs Lawson wrote, but lingered on in folk memory and the Goomstool Cottages beside the pond had kept their name, as had Stocks Yatt Lane, also the scene of mob justice and human misery.

Evil, actual or fancied, does seem to stir the mind and stay in the memory of the folk more than the pleasant or auspicious. Writing of Upton's chief villain, Captain Thomas Bound, she says: 'Our buildings and our politics, our customs and our fashions, are all changed since 1667; but the remembrance of this middle-class, middle-aged Puritan remains unaltered.' So hair-raising were the popular accounts of this landowner and participant in the Civil War – how he married three wives and made away with two, how cruel, covetous and hard on the poor he was, how he used to sneak about removing landmarks to the benefit of his own property, how he put a pen in the hand of a dead woman at Southend farmhouse and guided it 'so as her should sign a will which left all to him' and how, being haunted by the woman's ghost, he drowned himself in a pool and was denied Christian burial – she determined to dig the facts out from the parish records. Not one did she find to support the legend; all three of his wives had died naturally, the Southend farm he obtained on lease from the heir and the other lands he acquired were registered as having been fairly bought; and she concluded that his unpopularity arose from his heading the fanatical Puritan party in the parish which ousted a well-loved Rector, Mr Woodforde, an easy-going, conscientious and liberal man.

Slandering their betters may have been the only intellec-

117

tual pleasure known to these simple dishonest souls, but it brought a nemesis of its own. Their lurid imaginings took hold of their minds to such an extent that after his death they believed his wicked ghost still walked among them, doing all manner of harm; and their tales were handed down for generations, indeed to Mrs Lawson's own day, and terrified all who heard them.

I was amused by what Mrs Lawson had to say about collecting information from country people, because I have noted the same thing myself, even now. They cannot, she remarks, place any event, however important, in time unless it coincides with a happening in their own family. For example, 'That was when my father bought me a sweet pretty gown with blue roses on him, and 'twas the first as I had made long' or, 'That ere happened when our John, him as is married up the country was about cutting his first tooth.' Without an intimate knowledge of their personal concerns, it is difficult to sift information received in this way; and, in Mrs Lawson's case, there was a whole prehistoric period 'a very long time afore Mr Baines', without anyone explaining, or possibly knowing, who Mr Baines might have been.

Like a good Victorian church woman, she goes deeply into the condition of the poor, who were the responsibility of the parish and by no means loved in it. No effort was spared to prevent outsiders settling in Upton if they looked like becoming a charge and the homegrown feckless and the scroungers were given a rough ride too. Some families managed to make a career out of pauperism nevertheless, and even to found a pauper dynasty, for their names appear on the relief list regularly from 1682 to when Mrs Lawson wrote her book: in the early eighteenth century attempts were made to check this by making them wear a P (for pauper) on their week-day clothes, which shamed the innocent poor quite dreadfully and bothered the scroungers not at all. It was a far cry from our modern custom of handing out doles to all and sundry from Government funds which are impersonal and somehow unreal: a brisk battle of wits went on between the comfortably off and those with designs on their purses which makes lively reading in the parish records until the Upton workhouse opened in 1763. Then the poor, deserving or not, were swallowed up in it and their fascinating personal details with them.

Mrs Lawson was obliged to admit with sorrow that Upton had an evil reputation in the matter of drunkenness. 'Our town,' she writes, 'with a population of little over one thousand eight hundred, has at the present time nineteen public houses,' open all day, of course, no rubbish about permitted hours. Even then, her innate kindliness comes to the fore and she softens the charge by pointing out that drinking habits evolve from the customs of centuries, especially the customs of 'treating' and offering drink as part of wages. Men who refused it got no extra cash, so there was little inducement to do so even by those who really did not much care for it; and as for 'treating', it was done to everyone, high and low, including the Parson himself when he baptised a parish baby. There is an entry to this effect in the records, 'Spent in treating the Parson Jeffreys for baptizing the child, 1s.' Not bad at all, as a quart of ale at the time cost only twopence. And, although she does not mention this, for some reason waterside people, whether by sea or river, tend to drink more than the land-locked, something that can be noticed in Upton before. I have not counted the licensed establishments, as Mrs Lawson must have done, but they are plentiful, actually standing in a row along the river bank, and a good deal merrier than those in the country roundabout.

What comes out of this enchanting little book as clearly as the portrait of Upton is that of Emily Lawson herself, warm-hearted and charitable, devoted to the people, sharing in all their concerns and full of the insight which comes from sympathy. Victorians in general were often broader minded than we suppose, and she must have been exceptionally so, making allowances wherever she could; although it may be feared that the present state of our society might have been too much for even her.

Her husband the parson rounds the volume off with a glossary of Upton expressions, excluding such as 'belong to the domain of slang or coarse language or are used with uniform sound or meaning in most parts of England'; and he tells us that 'it is with a pang that some words and phrases have been omitted which belong to the Evesham neighbourhood'. The curious thing about it, however, is that his thirty-two pages are rife with words used not only in Evesham but all over England, and to this day: butty (work mate), cadge, carpet (call in for reproof), carryings-on, cowl (chimney top), dither, faddy, fetch (deal, as a blow), gaffer, handful (awkward person), kipe, moithered, off his head (out of his mind), perished (from cold etc.), sally (willow), tup (a ram), tussock, and so on, to pick out a random few. We can just see the dear fellow, busily making notes of them all as peculiar to his very own parish from which, one can only think, he seldom in his life had stirred, except as far as Evesham.

One 'remarkable tendency' in that neighbourhood, apparent to a less extent in Upton too, he does mention, and that is to decline the responsibility of a direct assertion and to guard against the possible consequences of any avowal. ' "Is your wife at home today, James?" "Well, sir, I shouldn't think but what 'er might be." ' This is not a 'remarkable tendency' at all, but one commonly found among rural folk, not only in England but everywhere else, reaching great heights in Ireland. 'There's maybe no such thing as the truth, ma'am,' an Irish workman suggested once as I strove to unravel a felony, 'and anyway, you mightn't believe it.' But in the excellent Parson's own words, 'these reminiscences must not be indulged, lest they run on for ever'; and we may leave him there, happily assured of the unique particularity and difference of the tiny patch of earth he inhabited.

Today, the most striking visual feature of Upton is a tower of red sandstone, all that remains of the old church formerly standing near the bridge. It is surmounted by a copper 'Doom' or 'Cupelow', put there at the suggestion of a churchwarden, vaguely inspired by St Peter's in Rome. It has to be said that there is no resemblance to St Peter's whatever, and the thing is frankly a bit of an eyesore. The ever-charitable Mrs Lawson maintains that, although an anachronism as perched on a fourteenth-century tower, it is not without architectural merit; but to others it looks for all the world like an oldfashioned pepperpot. It actually goes by that name in the town and the Upton correspondent of *Berrow's Journal*, a Worcester paper which claims to be the oldest in the world, signs his column with it; and, regarded with deep affection by all, it continues to lift its zany head to heaven, visible for miles around.

This is the only extravagance: the prevailing note is of decorous charm, thanks to the winding little streets of Georgian houses. By the time the Victorian era set in, Upton was no longer the thriving expanding centre it had been, and Victorian buildings are few, luckily. The Georgians thought of a street, a terrace or a square as a unity, not as a means of individual self-expression; and while Upton has outstanding examples of their art, such as the Water House or the Malt House near the river, what distinguishes it is the regular grace of the whole.

The High Street is particularly delightful, with inns, banks and shops in a comely row, all run by people anxious to please. The inns are comfortable and old-fashioned, but not self-consciously so, simply content to be themselves with no yearning for modern smartness. One of them, The Anchor, dates from the early seventeenth century, and The White Lion stands out for its grandiose façade and noble porch, surmounted by a lion. It also has the honour of having provided the background for a scene from *Tom Jones*, possibly where the young scamp takes a married lady for a splendid romp, frustrated alas by the arrival of her indignant husband. That seems to fit in best, but I cannot be sure. Mrs Lawson alludes to the fact but passes over it hurriedly, unwilling perhaps to let it be thought she ever had read the book: 'it can scarcely be considered a piece of history, national or parochial,' she remarks, and finds 'more worthy of note' that Mrs Siddons may once have acted in a backroom there.

I have an affection for The White Lion because on my first visit to Upton a young woman there was very kind to me. I had taken a bus from Malvern to Hanley Swan – or thought I had, on the driver assuring me that this was his destination – until all at once the Pepperpot came into view and I realized that something was wrong. The Upton road goes through Hanley Castle and the driver had mixed the two Hanleys up: he seemed to think this a natural error on his part and no cause for complaint on mine. It was raining fiercely that

121

afternoon, there would not be a bus to the Swan for a couple of hours and Upton could not boast of a single taxi. But a golden-hearted girl in The White Lion rang all the taxi firms in Malvern on my behalf and, when nothing came of that, showed me into a comfortable parlour to wait.

'Those drivers on the Gloucester route often don't know where they are going,' she remarked. 'There's quite a few like yourself get stranded here. Funny, when you think of it.'

With that, she bustled off and got me some tea, which she would take no payment for.

What gives piquancy – charm is perhaps not the word – to travel in England is that you never know what to expect from the people. Sturdy individuals to a man and a woman, there is no foretelling what their response will be. That bus driver, for example, felt no contrition for bringing me out of my way but, rather, that I ought to be grateful. Another man, he said, would have charged for the extra distance run. And had someone else been on duty in the Lion, or had I gone to another establishment, I might easily have met with a callous indifference, or with some inane proposal as to what I could do, or with a purely sadistic glee. This variety of temperament is not to be found in any other country I know, and certainly adds excitement to the day.

I next saw Upton under a very different aspect, on a beautiful sunny morning. The river, reflecting a cloudless sky, was blue and sparkling as the ocean, and all was lively and animated. Joggers of every age, size and shape were enjoying their singular pastime along the bank. The various craft were busy, sails were hoisted, sculls flashed in the air, now and then speedboats tore past, throwing out waves to rock the vessels all round, a dog paddled bravely after an owner who had tried to give him the slip ashore, and a girl tumbled into the water to shrieks of merriment from her companions.

There were three of us on this occasion with Bill the American, whose battered Rolls was always at the service of friends, and Oliver, a rosy-faced amiable Englishman with a deep devotion to and knowledge of the public houses of his native land. He soon disappeared into one of them, leaving Bill and me to explore by ourselves and plan the rest of the day. There were to be races in the afternoon on the course a little way from the town, not as grand or famous as Worcester or Cheltenham. I have always enjoyed small meetings for the pleasant family atmosphere, with everyone knowing everyone else and hailing old friends as they spotted them in the crowd, and I was all for going; but two jovial cynics we ran across put Bill against it. It is true that the race results at such places are often surprising, horses that ought to have won not even placed and the other way round, which had always seemed odd to a simpleton like myself; but I had never really analysed the fact. On hearing of our interest, the punters were ready with good advice.

'Don't you bet heavy, whatever you do,' they said. 'The jockeys are told when to hold back and when to let go. Too many wins are bad business. The owners can't afford 'em, not at these minor fixtures. It shortens the odds and they want to clean up on the Classics. So never bet on a horse because he's a good 'un. Don't think of the horse at all, it's the owner you want to watch.'

As often happens when a riddle is cleared up, the solution was so obvious that I marvelled to think it had never struck me. It was a new light on English racing, but it made sense of a kind, and if it came to studying form the owners could be as rewarding a subject as their beasts. Bill, as a betting man, took a materialist view, however, and urged that we skip the meeting. 'Sounds too much like Kentucky,' he explained. Our informants then renewed their offer to buy his vintage Rolls, the sight of which had brought us together, and this being politely refused we went our separate ways.

The meeting was described as the Bank Holiday one, although the holiday had been the day before. It was the third in a matter of weeks, and I had noted already how they stretched out at both ends in this part of the world, back to Thursday midday and forwards over Tuesday. Sometimes indeed, where Wednesday is early closing day, the people made a job of it and raked that in as well. The pace of industrial life, never feverish, grows steadily more relaxed, and perhaps at no far distant time in the Easter to Whitsun period they will join up one with another, and no one will do any work at all.

By now the little town was filling up with pleasure seekers from far and wide, all in the highest of spirits and, despite the national ruin, with plenty of cash to spend. We went back to the High Street inn where Oliver was installed, placidly drinking his beer and observing the motley crowd, unmistakeable Upton regulars and carefree visitors off the boats. I was glad to see that dogs were welcome here, for a nasty habit of shutting them out is taking hold in all too many places. This may be due to the influence of American tourists who bring their fancies with them, one being that all dogs are ridden with fleas. Even if that were true, no flea in its senses would leave a warm fragrant furry coat for a cool antiseptic hairless body like theirs; and dogs moreover are well-conducted, seldom raise their voices and never chew gum.

A troop of Americans doing both had followed us in. They had come from Gloucester, having heard that a pig was to be roasted whole in the King's Head square; and they were much put out to find that this had happened the day before. No doubt they were filled with dreams of a slap-up barbecue with sauces and side-dishes, and the homely slices of pork clapped between doorsteps of bread would have disappointed them greatly. This they could not know, however, and they were inclined to be querulous: it was not the first time they had been misled and they were working a case up against the nation.

'You folks never know what's going on, or where,' one growled. 'Don't you *wawnt* any tourists?'

As a matter of act we did not, or not this kind. The one who objected to them most strongly was Bill the expatriate or, as he put it, the refugee. It was too bad, he muttered, that having escaped from their like at home he should find them closing in on him here. If it was all the same to us, he would rather we changed our plans and went on to lunch at Tewkesbury. These people always moved around in coachloads and in a place this size we should knock into them wherever we went. And let them but hear him speak and he was lost. 'Hi, you're American, what State you from, Oklahoma? For heaven's sake, so'I, what do you know!' And then photographs of the kids back home or themselves in front of

Buckingham Palace, and complaints of everything everywhere.

Until I met Bill, I had always supposed that dodging one's fellow countrymen was a purely English habit. I was too much given that way myself not to feel sympathy with him, and Oliver never cared where we went as long as the beer was good. Years ago he had discovered that the traditional ale at the Hop Pole Inn was sound, and ever since that was what Tewkesbury had stood for in his mind. He agreed at once to the change of plan and only said, we ought to look sharp in case the licensing hours of Gloucester were different from those of Worcester.

Chapter Thirteen

Tewkesbury is even more plentifully supplied with inns than Upton, all ancient and attractive, and the enumeration of them takes nearly as much space in the *Shell Guide* as the details of the great Norman Abbey. To mention a few, there is the Bell, which started life as a thirteenth-century monastic guest-house and still has wall paintings from the seventeenth century: the Swan, of course, Swans are rife in this part of the world: the Tudor House, which has a priest-hole in one of the chimneys: the old Black Bear, which claims to have carried on business since 1308; and the Hop Pole itself, where Mr Pickwick and the two rowdy young medicos paused to wine and dine on their errand of diplomacy to the cantankerous old Mr Winkle. The traditional ale of which Oliver approved may have been much the same as that which, helped by Madeira and port, put Mr Pickwick to sleep for thirty miles of the onward journey and caused Weller and Sawyer to sing duets in the coach dickey.

Seeing this cheerful thriving house reminded me of the *Papers*, and a prophecy concerning them which I happened to have recently found in a highly serious and edifying work by a Scottish theologian. The worthy man, a Mr Henry Drummond, was writing on St Paul's famous letter to the Corinthians about the nature of love; and when he reached the words 'Where there be tongues, they shall fail', he got rather carried away. How true this was, he cried, Greek and Latin were gone, Indian was going, the speech of Wales, Ireland and the Scottish Highlands was dying before our eyes; and, he continued, 'The most popular book in the English tongue today, except for the Bible, is one of Dickens's works, *The Pickwick Papers*. It is largely written in the language of London street life; and experts assure us that in fifty years it will be unintelligible to the average English

126

reader.' Drummond was writing this in 1911 – so much for experts and, perhaps, for Scottish theologians as well.

My companions hurried into the Hop Pole at once, for valuable drinking time had been lost on the road. We agreed to go our separate ways from now until we went home, our aims and interests being different. Bill did not want to visit the Abbey because he had seen it before: he had ticked it off in his mind as something over and done with, an American habit I find very strange. Do they never re-read a book or go to an opera twice? Most likely not. Oliver, on the other hand, never wanted to see, or read, or hear, anything of an improving nature at all and fed his mind entirely on its inner resources. They had some idea, when the bar should close, of hiring a motorboat and going up the Avon towards Evesham, thirty odd miles away. It was not, however, for the sake of the glorious country through which they would pass: Oliver wished to commune with himself in peace until 'they' opened again, and Bill loved any new sort of engine.

Leaving them to their lucubrations, I walked up to the Abbey. In this region of noble church building, it is hard to pick out the finest, Worcester, Hereford and Gloucester Cathedrals, Malvern Priory, all having their own special beauties, but for me Tewkesbury Abbey carries away the palm. That Norman sturdiness combined with delicacy, the huge rotund pillars and sweeping arches together with such exquisite detail, are overwhelming. This place too, like all those others, is alive with ghosts, but nothing could be less creepy; and today it looked more enchanting than ever as a flower festival was being held. The lovely proportions of the Lady Chapel were accentuated by the careful choice and placing of flowers in it and there were bursts of colour everywhere against the pale stone of the interior.

The atmosphere was especially delightful altogether. Some one was dreamily playing the organ, and women busy at various tasks gave me a friendly smile as I went by. The quiet good manners of church attendants in England are a boon to those accustomed to the harangues of guides and the importuning of hucksters abroad. They are educated people, of course, giving their services for love and having no need to look on the visitor as prey, and it makes a world of difference

127

to the enjoyment. Far from being pestered to buy postcards or address-books or little gold crosses, one often cannot find people to take the money for them: very often there is only a box left trustingly on the stall. And here, among the more usual knick-knacks, there was a basket of fine brown eggs and a trug of crisp lettuce left over from a fete and with a pleasantly rural air about them.

Although there are hints of High Church tendencies, as in so many great Anglican centres now, the Abbey has escaped the rash of pictures and statues that has frequently broken out elsewhere. It is odd how, while Catholic taste is more and more for the plain and austere, the Anglicans have begun to indulge a fondness for clutter; but here all is still mercifully bare, with little to distract the eye from the splendid lines of the building. The many tombs and monuments commemorating the great families of the region, de Clares, Warwicks and de Spensers are wholly in keeping with their background. One of great charm is the tomb, or chantry of Edward Baron de Spenser, who held a high command under the Black Prince at Poitiers in 1350 and was the tenth Knight of the Garter. The effigy is of stone, a figure kneeling above the chantry itself and facing the High Altar in a posture said to be unique. It is in full armour, the mail-gloved hands pressed devoutly together and only the face with its strong dark brows and moustache, its full red mouth and formidable nose left unprotected. It is not an English face at all but one that is still to be seen in parts of Normandy, reminding us that the foundations for the hostility felt for us by the French were securely laid by their fellowcountrymen. The Baron's eyes are fierce and strangely alive, and he looks altogether more likely to be at home on a battlefield than in his present abode. But he is a general favourite with the people of Tewkesbury, who make a point of asking if the stranger has admired him.

Less of an eye-catcher but very fine is the Warwick Chantry, put up by the Countess of Warwick in memory of her first husband, before she married Warwick the Kingmaker – a name cropping up continually in centuries of history and tradition. It was at Tewkesbury that one of the bitterest blows to the Lancastrian side in the Wars of the Roses was dealt in

1417. Emboldened by the death of the Kingmaker at Barnet, Margaret of Anjou, wife of Henry VI, had determined to make a final desperate stand; but her commander, the Duke of Somerset, was easily outclassed by the Yorkists under Edward IV and her troops were routed with horrible carnage in a field still known as Bloody Meadow. And bloody was the word for that whole pack of miscreants, all clamouring alike for St George to defend their own particular view of the right while they slaughtered, pillaged and double-crossed in their frantic struggle for power.

Now some of that angry dust lies peacefully buried in the chapels of the Abbey. After contemplating the monuments awhile, I toiled up to the roof of the tower to enjoy the lovely view over the Severn and Avon valleys and the Malvern hills. On this bright afternoon there was even a glimpse of shadowy masses far away to the west, which a fellow traveller assured me were the Mendip range. I said that surely they must be the mountains of Wales, an error of judgement, as he had the long obstinate sheepish face that goes with a dislike of contradiction. He replied vehemently that I was wrong and there could be no doubt at all of their being the Mendips.

'And I ought to know,' he added: 'That's where I come from.'

Having settled the point in this conclusive fashion, he proceeded to misinform me about various other landmarks in the panorama, pointing them out with his stick like the British tourist who had so disgusted Francis Kilvert. He was clearly one of those male pests who feel obliged to harangue and bore any woman they find alone. I stood it as patiently as I could until he started putting questions to make sure I had taken his lecture in and then I glumly went away.

The Abbey grounds set the building off most beautifully, with their lofty old dark trees and vivid grass, carefully tended but not so much as to behead the hosts of cheerful little daisies around the tombs. These are ancient, sunk in the earth, their contours softened by time and weather, with one exception, of all incongruous things a monument to relations of Barbara Cartland, the romantic novelist. How on earth had she managed that, I wondered, and what did the de Clares,

129

de Spensers and Beauchamps make of it all? Here too I met a familiar type but a pleasanter one, a matronly figure with easel and paintbox, sketching away with firm resolute strokes, her large straw hat kept in place by a bandeau tied under her chin, as ladies secured their hats in the early days of the motor car. I crept a little nearer to get a peep at the sketch which was exactly like all the sketches I ever saw produced by this school, not a ha'porth of difference between them. Musing on this and wondering what became of them all when finished, I did not notice that she in turn was having a long steady look at me; and it came as a surprise when she suddenly opened her mouth and uttered the two words, 'Lemon curd!'

'Sorry?'

'Lemon curd. Don't you remember? Surely you must remember?'

And then I did. We had met before in a Ledbury teashop, she being with friends, tweedy self-assured ladies like herself. They had asked for lemon curd which was not to be had, and this resulted in lamentation, an exhaustive discussion of the delicacy and the various methods of making it, and finally, the instant formation of a Lemon Curd Club. All of them were of that public-spirited Tory breed that revels in clubs and committees, but they were also unconventional enough to invite me, a stranger, to join it: so that while I had been watching her as a naturalist watches a specimen, she had promptly recognized me as a fellow lemon curdist.

'Ah yes, of course. How is the Club?'

'It flourishes,' she replied briefly, and went back to her work. She was not sketching the Abbey at all but a picturesque old house over the way, having merely settled herself with a memsahib's assurance wherever was convenient.

There was another of this hardy sisterhood in the Information office nearby, where I looked in to collect a plan of the town. The office had a guichet opening on to a bus-stop shelter with a wooden bench running round it; and on this sat a dishevelled man, either drunk or mad, who brandished a bottle between bursts of manic laughter. The office lady, fresh-faced and smart in her mauve twinset and pearls, answered my questions calmly and briskly, with that sublime unawareness of anything up which characterizes the race. She was junior to the artist by many years, and it was heartening to see that the strain was not dying out.

Time had been marching on meanwhile, and I was hungry. Sounds of popular rejoicing came from one of the old taverns down the street and, hurrying to it, I found a landlord with a most enlightened disregard for the law. The question I put to him was of the sort usual among our cowed and dispirited people, which fairly begs for a damping reply: 'I suppose I'm too late for anything now?' 'Never too late,' he responded, 'as long as you have the money.' And he set before me a Ploughman's Lunch and a glass of wine, expressing the hope that I would enjoy them. It was one more case of serendipity. Notices were prominently displayed saying that youngsters could not be served and small children not allowed in at all, but the place was full of teenagers swigging their vodka or beer and happy little tots creating a hullabaloo. I must not name this well-disposed establishment, but it has left a pleasant memory.

There are many good indoor things in this little town, painting, panelling, a fine museum, of which the people are justly proud, but on so radiant an afternoon I preferred to ramble about in the open. It is very pleasant, too, to come on attractive places haphazardly rather than make out a list of what should be seen. One of them was the old Mill down by the river set in a beautiful corner with the Abbey tower in the background, and with that quietly important air that mills always have. And there was the house of the Nodding Gables, which I spotted at once from the Shell Guide's remark that its appearance was consonant with its name. It did indeed look on the point of nodding off altogether, but this condition is so usual among houses throughout the region as hardly to call for special note.

Presently I found myself on the bank of the Avon once more, and looked out for my two companions, who might by now be returning from their maiden voyage. There was no sign of them, but the activity on the water was an entrancing show as always. To mess about in boats or watch others doing it is indeed one of the pleasures of life. The people here

131

seemed to be quiet and more experienced than the merry raffish crowd at Upton, and the river itself moved with a placid dignity unlike the ebullient Severn.

Once it had been a slow drowsy stream of varying depth, unfit for vessels of any size. Then a landowner, William Sandys, thought to do the Vale of Evesham and himself some good by converting it into a waterway from Tewkesbury to Warwick, putting a stop to their dependence on the Severn. He was granted a licence by Charles I in 1635 and went to work, only to run into difficulties with his labourers, who were not unlike those of the present time. The job was too hard and too dirty to please them, and they refused to turn out in winter at all. The Civil War broke out before they had got to Evesham and poor Sandys never reaped the rewards of his effort; but the undertaking went forward again with the Commonwealth and struggled as far as Stratford after the Restoration. But the new backer, Lord Windsor, felt that enough had been spent on the project, and that was that. Shipping never got to Warwick, but there was a good trade run from Bristol to Evesham for two hundred years until railways took the business from water routes everywhere. So that it has become once more a quiet stretch of clean water, flowing past mills and churches and woods and meadows, triumphantly useless and a refreshment to the soul.

I was drinking in the delightful scene when a wild-looking individual accosted me. Either he was athirst for conversation, or he could not bear to see anyone enjoying herself in peace. He began by asking if I were a stranger, which led me to fear that he might be yet another of Kilvert's monsters, about to point out the local attractions with his stick. Not a bit of it: for on hearing that I was he went on to say, 'Then you can have no idea how much of this land has been filched from the people.' Filched? By whom? 'By *them*,' he replied, and recited a whole inventory of what had been seized, not only here but as far off as the Hanleys and Malvern itself. He spoke with such fire and fervour, it sounded as if it had happened just the other day, and it seemed odd that I had heard nothing whatever about it, a scandal so outrageous, it could topple a government or even the whole regime. But what he had in mind, as eventually came out, were the Enclosure Acts of the eighteenth century.

I could not but warm to this single-minded man. There was something infectious about his noble rage. And to find that particular sort in one of our own people was a novel experience. While the Irish harp on Cromwell, the Spaniards explode at the mention of Henry VIII, even the rational French heat up over the Maid of Orleans, most of us leave the past to bury its dead. Yet here was a run-of-the-mill Saxon, in cloth cap, open shirt and sneakers, a pigeon fancier or skittle champion in his spare time you would have said, for whom the past and present were one!

The drawback, as so often, was that I saw no chance of getting away. By now he had moved on to the Worcester area, revealing the same breadth of knowledge as before. I muttered something about there being two sides to a question, a red herring that usually works, but he seemed not to hear. 'Take Madresfield,' he cried passionately, 'Madresfield now, there's a . . .' At this point, however, help suddenly came from outside.

'Alf!' The speaker stood a little way off, a large woman in flowered print and lacy cardigan, with wife written all over her. 'Supposed to be buying the meat and here he is down by the river making a show of himself again while the rest of us wait for 'is majesty in the car.' She was not addressing me, merely summing things up for an unseen presence in whom she was wont to confide. 'No thought for others. Ho no.'

'I was just telling the lady, dear . . .'

'I daresay. Come along, do.' Turning on her heel she marched away, followed by the deprecating Alf. Snatches of wifely comment drifted back to me through the peaceful air as they went. I could see that he was going to catch it, and the saddest part was that his suffering would all be vain for I could not remember a single word he said.

Boats were coming in and tying up by now as evening approached, and there was still no sign of my friends. The best idea would be to go back to the Hop Pole, where sooner or later like roosting birds they were bound to fly in. And indeed as I went into the bar there the two of them sat, in the very same places, as if they had never stirred at all. They were both in high feather. Although the afternoon had not turned out according to plan, it had been very much to their

133

taste. On the way to look for a motor launch, the Rolls had broken down and Bill had spent some blissful hours poking about in her innards while Oliver snoozed on the back seat: both felt that they could not have put their time to better use.

'And would you believe it,' said Bill, 'I got that engine working within minutes of opening time!'

'Providential,' Oliver gravely agreed. 'It must have been meant.'

They had ordered a meal of Dickensian scope, on the grounds that I must be famished, and then ate it nearly all themselves. It was decided that Oliver should take the wheel homeward, he being one of those men that could probably drive under a general anaesthetic. As an extra precaution, he put on a chauffeur's cap and tunic, while Bill and I sat behind, in bourgeois respectability. They had reckoned long ago that police would not carry out a random check on a chauffeur-driven car, and had travelled freely ever since, immune as Arab diplomats. A wide-awake copper might have queried the combination of museum Rolls and chauffeur, especially as the latter wore trousers of dog's-tooth tweed, but there must have been none about, for all we passed only gave us a look of friendly amusement. Under Oliver's capable hands the old girl darted through the crowded streets like a minnow and out in a flash on to the Worcester road; and Bill enlivened the journey for me with a detailed account of what had gone wrong and how he had set it to rights.

Chapter Fourteen

Another rainy spell had set in and as my next visit was to
Stratford-on-Avon, which called for fine weather, I kicked
my heels in Worcester until it should pass. There were things
to be attended to, correspondence of which more anon, and
my hair, a fast and furious growth that needed pruning every
week if I was to look respectable, and which had been let rip
for over a month. The boy who cut it frankly confessed he
hardly knew where to begin, suggesting that it might be
more manageable if allowed to grow to shoulder-length and
tied back with a ribbon, like his own; but I rejected this as too
youthful, and also masculine, and bade him do the best he
could.

I mention this homely affair because in the course of
conversation he made a strange and interesting remark. On
the way to his salon I had met some teenagers with their hair
dyed in vivid shades of purple, green and pink, and thought
I should get a professional view of this practice. Nigel, as his
name was, knew all about it, the dyes they used, how often
they applied them, the hazard of dermatitis and so on; and
when I asked him why they did it, he told me that they were
affirming their identity as original human beings.

Like the rest of us, I have heard a deal of nonsense about
this matter of identity. It seems to be a major preoccupation
of our time. At one moment hardly a novel appeared in
America whose hero was not busily searching for his own;
and I always thought it rather absurd, because people either
know who they are, in which case they need not worry or
they do not, and then are unlikely ever to find out. But to
know, or at any rate feel, that you are blessed with originality
and to affirm it by dying your hair orange or pink, or both, in
company with scores of others, struck me as absurdity of a
very special kind. I could have wished to inquire further, to

135

ask if this originality manifested itself in other ways as well, but Nigel had spoken so gravely and conclusively, on the whole it seemed better not.

In the days that followed, I noticed a change of attitude in myself. To begin with, I had been thinking of this country mainly in terms of others, as travellers do even of their own, and having lived so long in Ireland and Spain had been struck by the differences between them, the relative efficiency and order here. But now I was growing acclimatized and beginning to compare the state of the nation with what it had been formerly, when a return from the Continent meant a stepping up to a noticeably higher level of civilization.

Seen in this new perspective, it did look rather different. The pile of correspondence which had accumulated in my absence was a social study in itself. There was so much of it that I might have been a flourishing one-woman business, but many of the items need never have been sent at all: for example, a crop of solicitations from mail order firms who had got my name and address by some crafty means were thrown away unread. Then there were those which ought not to have been written and for which a computer was to blame. It has often been explained to me that computers are no sillier than the people who work them, but I deny this: there is a malign imbecility about their efforts which a human being alone could never hope to rival. Here were the usual demands for payments long since made, including one which threatened me with the law if a sum of £ nil nil p was not received within eight days. They say, if you send a cheque for these phantom sums the mindless brute will hold its peace, but I don't see why we should pander to it.

Speaking of cheques brings to mind another feature of present-day correspondence, this time a purely human one. 'Enclosed please find our cheque . . . ' a letter runs, and there is nothing we should like better, but the cheque is not there. The gnome who should have seen to it was thinking of other things or perhaps not thinking at all. I don't know what the psychological term for it is, alienation possibly, or dissociation, but secretaries now often take down and type out letters mechanically, without heed to their sense. 'Thank you for notifying us of your new address', they write, and send the acknowledgement off to the old one. The employer says nothing, either because he has not noticed or, more likely, because he is afraid. Fear of underlings seems to hold the nation in its grip: it is remarkable how politicians and journalists who fearlessly call for a stand against Russia or a strong line with the unions are perfect jelly-fish with their own staff. And unlike the mail order firms and the computers, these slapdash people involve you in correspondence yourself, wasting your time, burdening the mails and giving the Post Office another excuse for putting its charges up.

Having weeded all this out, I turned to the handful of letters that remained and was interested to find one that had taken eleven days in transit from Cornwall. This was a further point of difference from days gone by, and by that I do not mean those of my youth but of much further back. Again and again in Victorian novels the speed with which letters moved about England comes up, and always as something to be taken for granted. Wilkie Collins was an author who took no liberties with fact, and the plot of *The Moonstone* requires that a letter posted in Yorkshire should be delivered in London by nine-thirty next morning without fail and the reply to it reach Yorkshire on the following day. What writer of the present time would dare to hinge his story on anything so preposterous? And what, pray, was my Cornwall letter doing in those eleven days? Someone could have brought it to Worcester on foot in half the time. It was all the stranger because two other communications, one from Malaga and one from Tokyo, had taken three and six days respectively.

Worthy of mention too, perhaps, was a postcard from a friend in London who was coming to Worcester and asked to be met at the station. The postmark had been heavily stamped on the very time of arrival, blotting it out for ever. As it was not a picture card but a plain one, with the address and the message on different sides, this had an air of deliberate censorship; but no doubt it was simply the work of one more dissociated gnome, with his mind far away on football or sex.

This dreaminess was not confined to postal clerks or secretaries or other people operating at a distance, but was often met in personal transactions. The younger staff generally

137

seemed to have little grasp of or interest in what they were doing. Did I ask for some well-known book in what appeared to be a thriving store, for example, ten to one the assistant had never heard of it: or had heard of it and was 'always being asked for it', although obviously in vain; and there was the helpful young woman who was unable to supply a Barbara Pym but could 'do' me a Barbara Cartland instead, much as in Lipton's of Gibraltar an inquiry for Gentleman's Relish is answered with polite regrets and an offer of Horse Radish. And when you went to pick up your dry-cleaning, on which an Express Service fee had been paid, perhaps it had not come in, or had come in but was not to be found, so would you call again in the afternoon or tomorrow? Or, having waited twenty minutes for a cup of coffee, you might be asked by a cheerful waitress, 'What was your order again?' Even buying a railway ticket was not the simple affair it had been once, when the ticket and your change were slapped down together almost before you had finished speaking, because now the vendor had to look up the price in some reference work which might be in use elsewhere or mislaid.

At times I really felt I was in the Balkans, and I began to see that the taxi boy in Chester who thought his job was merely to drive, not to know the way to anywhere, was no isolated phenomenon but part of a national movement. Only his grumpiness was peculiar to himself, and due perhaps to his having been obliged to leave his bed so early, because all these young people were as relaxed and friendly as could be; and there were few signs of impatience from the victims, whatever their age, as if all this were a fact of modern life, like inflation.

It was in the field of public works that the sign of new times could be most vividly appreciated. In private businesses there would often be some harassed relict of a former age who might be appealed to in extremity, but the merry men of roads, water, electricity or telephones seemed to be quite on their own. You might pass a group of half a dozen or so of whom two were digging a hole in the ground for some purpose, while the rest looked on, and returning that way later you would find the hole much the same size and the task force seated in their lorry, listening to the radio

138

and drinking tea. A man up a telegraph pole evidently needed two colleagues to hold the ladder and shout up encouragement and advice. A band of toilers about to tar a small patch of road would first consult together for half an hour or so, as if they had never tackled this kind of problem before.

A striking feature about these activities was that there seemed to be no gaffer, no one person in command. Those taking part were like a committee without a chairman, groping its way toward consensus by fraternal discussion without any casting vote. It was a system that had been tried in Russia once but long given up, as hours went by with the workers merely repeating what they had said already. What the theory behind it here may have been, I cannot imagine: most likely there was none, merely the facts of being paid by the hour, a union ready to cut up rough at the very mention of productivity, and a helpless public to foot the bill; but the debates were carried out in high good humour and comfortable air of time being no object, an air in harmony with the physique of many engaged, who looked more like budding aldermen than honest working lads.

It must have been pleasant for all concerned, but the question seemed to be how long it could continue. How long could the public sector hold up with, say, four men doing the work of one? I asked myself – unless their wages were cut by three quarters, and the mind fairly reeled to think of that. Were the powers responsible walking in their sleep? Would they awake one day to find the money all gone and grim reality staring them in the face? A vision troubled me of those blithe young Billy Bunters herded into Government relief camps, or diving for coins thrown by compassionate tourists. The prospect seemed wild and remote enough, but I feared it, I feared it greatly.

Chapter Fifteen

The fine weather returned in due course, suddenly and with the usual wide innocent smile as if it had never been away. The drive through the Vale of Evesham was beautiful, past fields and orchards, may and chestnut trees in pink or crimson flower, newly opened beech buds of dazzling green, here and there a poplar, its bright yellow leaves twinkling and shivering in the sun. All along the road there was country produce for sale, farm eggs, flowers cut or for planting, lettuces, baby chicks. What looked like a huge lake with its ripples frozen over turned out to be a strawberry farm, with the fruit ripening under acres of plastic cloches. Then back to mile after mile of apples and pears, until all at once on a particularly English looking hill, grassy slopes with a crest of woodland, there was a brave exotic show, a troop of splendid Palomino horses, their bodies the colour of Arabian sand, mane and tail of cream, with a leggy foal or two capering awkwardly round them.

Our coach had left fifteen minutes late, in accordance – as I had come to see – with local practice; and the driver smoked unmercifully all the way. Beast! as the Reverend Francis Kilvert would doubtless have remarked. He was a man of special gifts, however, for as he drove and despite the cigarette he talked loudly and without stopping to a man in the front seat. There was the usual notice forbidding anyone to speak to or distract him, which was complied with more or less, as the other hardly got a word in; but the disregard of the no-smoking rule, which I had thought peculiar to Latins and Greeks, was complete and barefaced. Perhaps this too was common practice now, or perhaps he felt himself above the law, for he certainly had a sense of his own importance. On arrival I asked him when he would be going back in the evening, and he replied with dignity, 'I shall not be going back at all'; and as we walked away I overheard him telling a mate that tomorrow was his *birthday*, in tones that suggested red letters in the calendar. But he stood about five foot two or three, which may have accounted for this.

A modern theatre had been built since last I was here, and catching sight of a hideous squat erection on the way to the town centre I feared that this might be it; but, as I should have guessed, it was the Hilton Hotel. People say harsh things about the Hilton chain and indeed every one of them known to me is a fright, each in its particular way; but they do a useful service by drawing into themselves, poultice-fashion, a tribe that one would be sorry to see at large. This is of special value in a cultural Mecca like Stratford and deserves to be set off against the horrid appearance.

The sun was beaming on the pleasant little town. There were more chestnut trees in flower lining the road to the theatre, which had a fine approach of lawns and rose trees. Crowds of birds swam to and fro on the river, regally, placidly, saucily, according to their breed, swans, ducks, moorhen, most of them with chicks following in their wake. There seemed a considerable change in the human element as I remembered it, those earnest males with their beards, sandals and cloaks, the females beardless but similarly garbed with long earrings and Indian bangles added, being apparently extinct. Their successors were such as might be found on any Bank Holiday at Hampstead Heath, lolling in chairs or lying about on the grass, drinking Coca Cola and munching crisps, and none really looked as if Shakespeare was his favourite author. Beards there were in plenty, but here again was a difference. Formerly these were a kind of badge, denoting a taste for art or a penchant for Leftwing politics, marking the wearer as anti-bourgeois, anti-Philistine, anti-Establishment, a thinker and superior person altogether: now they suggested no more than a simple reluctance to shave, borne out by the frayed jeans, grubby hands and oniony smell of sweat that accompanied them. Certainly they indicated no desire to improve or reform the world, which seemed greatly to their owners' liking as it was, for a more relaxed and jovial crowd would have been difficult to imagine.

The theatre providing a back-cloth for this merry scene was suitably imposing, with the whiff of mausoleum about it that goes with institutions of the kind. The company was to perform *Twelfth Night* that evening, in the traditional manner it seemed. In London they had tried to freshen up this ever-fresh comedy by means of stale gimmickry: photographs in the hall showed the Lady Olivia in skin tights and a tunic open to reveal her bosom, a curious ensemble for an Elizabethan woman of rank, the head of a large household, pious and in mourning. What would this enterprising crew be up to next? I asked myself in trepidation: Prince Hal and Hotspur transmogrified into Hell's Angels, may be, Hamlet a mole in Norwegian pay, Lady Macbeth, maligned victim of PMT, Othello, maddened by race discrimination, his doings a cry for help – the possibilities were endless.

I wondered too why directors should take liberties with Shakespeare and not with authors of the Restoration, say, whose wigs and swords and buckled shoes appear to be sacrosanct. Perhaps they feel the Restoration theatre is of that period only, while Shakespeare is for ever; but paradoxically, a true contemporary setting brings out his timelessness the more, while modern dressing merely takes away from it.

Another grumble of mine about Shakespearian productions of the present day is the awful English that younger players often speak. Nowhere does the generation gap make itself more acutely felt, or more absurdly, because the cleavage goes right through the cast regardless of the characters being played. Desdemona's nurse will speak like a gentlewoman while Desdemona herself sounds like a shopgirl: young noblemen rattle on in the grisly accents appropriate to Bottom the Weaver or Dogberry the policeman. And no producer dare pull them up, no critic pans them as he should, for fear of being called a snob, a word by the way which has practically lost all meaning. In any case, diction in the theatre is not a matter of class but of getting things right. An actor playing a gentleman should speak like one, walk, sit down and get up like one, and if he does not know how he should learn, just as he would learn to do as an Indian doctor does, or an Irish gunman, if he were playing that. The late lamented Edith Evans came of fairly modest origins but no one could sound more regal if her part required it and her speech was a delight to the ear.

There is a definite, rather aggressive, social theory behind the uncritical modern approach, of course. Since educated people no longer rank as better than others, it follows that their accent cannot do so either, whatever our ears may tell us. And it goes beyond the matter of pronunciation too: there is to be no hard-and-fast rule in points of stress, the individual placing it where he chooses, although our ears tell us again that the rhythm is thereby ruined. I have heard a budding Hamlet from a school of drama declaim:

> Ow, vat vis tew tew SOLID flesh would me-oot,
> Faw, AND resohlve itse-oof into a dew ...

which would hardly have met with Shakespeare's approval. Indeed, if his plays have remained comprehensible and delightful to the passing generations it was precisely because rules were kept, lines scanning and words rhyming as they should; and if this free-for-all continues the time may come when audiences hardly understand what is being said. That may sound a little extreme, but I have been assured by the pronunciation unit of the BBC that 'modern linguisticians, of course, would never speak of "mistakes in English"' which, if true, must surely end in chaos.

But enough of these sombre thoughts, which have little to do with the Bard's birthplace. He certainly appeared to be a money-spinner there, if nothing else. There were shops upon shops, antique dealers, boutiques, Asian bazaars, Chinese take-aways, as well as good English firms displaying their tweed, porcelain or sporting equipment, and others of a baser kind, full of unbelievable trash, knick-knacks and souvenirs such as no one in his senses would ever want to buy. In particular I observed a collection of white clay pipes for blowing bubbles, one of which I bought to prove to myself that I had not been dreaming.

It cost £1.25: everything here seems to cost more than anywhere else, as if Shakespeare's birthplace felt authorized to impose a special tax on all who came near it. There were

143

some of those Indian skirts that apparently are made of butter muslin offered at 'only' £5.99 and which were going at £3.25 in Malvern, itself no bargain centre; but when this was pointed out to the vendor, he hid behind a sudden ignorance of the English vernacular.

I was mug enough to pay £1 for admission to the Elizabethan Pageant, in a small round theatre with only eight seats provided, all mugs above that number being obliged to stand for the same price of admission. These seats were built to swivel round like an office chair, because the various scenes took place in little cells built into the circular wall, lighting up one after the other. Now we saw the Queen addressing the loyal citizens, now a scene of plague, now some historic confrontation or notorious crime, now the Queen descending on some unfortunate bigwig, whom she and an ample retinue were to honour with an extended stay. Oh yes, and of course there was Shakespeare's father, the glove merchant, making a fuss of a little boy called Will. It was awful enough to be funny, like Hollywood at its most pretentious, and, like Hollywood's cultural efforts, mounted regardless of expense.

From there I went on to recruit my forces in one of the many attractive inns with Shakespearian names or references that are dotted about the town. These have a genuine old flavour about them, inside and out, and the owners have the sense not to put the staff into period costume. Nor, in the one I happened to pick on, was there a waiter anything like Francis, with his cheerful 'Anon, anon, sir!' to thirsty and impatient customers: you fetched your own drink from a bar presided over by a disciplinarian in a purple velvet dress, her hair dyed a malignant yellow. No sooner was I comfortably settled on a bench by the window, with an admirable view of the passersby, than she left her bar and came across, remarking sternly, 'You can't bring your feud in here.'

I couldn't immediately think what she meant, unless my face was still working away with the indignation caused by the pageant, and so I asked, 'What feud?'

'I didn't say feud, I said feud,' she snapped. 'We serve feud in our boofy, so no one can't bring in their own.'

She was glaring at the crusty ham roll I had bought in a

delicatessen and was now taking out of its paper. I offered to buy one of hers if she would leave me to the enjoyment of mine, a sporting offer to which she deigned no reply. What could have brought this aggressive little London sparrow so far from her natural surroundings, in Praed Street perhaps or Soho? The hope of catching a producer's eye and treading the boards as Cleopatra? Not only the opulent dress but the consequence of manner hinted at some such dream, and marked her out as at any rate too fine to draw beer.

'Where is the boofy, then?' I asked with resignation, putting the sandwich roll away.

'Down the passage, can't miss it, it's wrote up on the door,' she said. 'On'y it's shut today,' she added cheerfully. 'Shuts on a Monday, the boofy does.'

I drank up, marvelling, and went away to eat my lunch on a seat by the river. Near that was a landing stage with a board announcing trips on a motor launch, and presently I joined one of these. It turned out to be the most agreeable part of the day: the water was deliciously dappled by sun and shade as we chugged along beneath the trees on the bank, and it threw wavy patterns on their trunks and leaves: it was like some lovely Impressionist painting. After a while the trees came to an end and we passed by a series of flower gardens, imaginatively planted and beautifully kept, each with a house of patrician aspect. In one of them a lady, gloved and with a wide straw hat, was delicately snipping off dead flowers and dropping them into a basket, in another, an old gentleman of distinguished appearance repeatedly threw a ball for a little dog, in a third, a gardener stood resting himself with a hand to the small of his back. They never turned their heads as we went splashing by, as if what happened in the world outside their garden could be of no interest: all was calm and dignified in this tourist-free part of the town.

There was nothing tourist-free about the launch itself, however. It contained a party of Germans in Lederhosen and Alpine hats, who possessed the usual carrying voices of their tribe. They were arguing about something or other, as usual again, and were becoming steadily more vociferous. It was impossible not to hear what they said; and, strange as it

145

might appear in such surroundings, they were going hammer and tongs into the question of who wrote Shakespeare. The loudest of the group was evidently the least sure of his ground, for he decided to rope me in.

'I am sure you agree,' he began in awful English, 'that the greatest of poets was Lord Bacon?'

'I think it was probably Shakespeare,' I replied. 'But in any case there was no Lord Bacon.'

'*No Lord Bacon?*'

'There was a Master Francis Bacon who ended up as Lord Verulam. But I cannot believe that he wrote the plays.'

He bridled at this. 'You perhaps cannot believe that a lawyer should be also a poet?'

Aha, that was it! The poor fellow had *Rechtsanwalt* written all over him. I had been trying to account for the interest taken by one who was unable or would not bother even to speak Shakespeare's language well.

'I don't say that,' I told him pacifically. 'Bacon was a very fine author, but the playwright had an altogether different voice. I have never understood how anyone might confuse them.'

'*Was sagt sie?*' put in one of the others.

'*Lauter Quatsch,*' snapped the lawyer. 'What you say is very interesting,' he continued to me. 'But in Chermany there are many *men*, clever *men*, who are convinced that it must be as I propose. Myself has studied this problem for many years. And I am President of a Lord Bacon Society,' he added, as if that clinched the matter once and for all.

I could think of no suitable reply to this and so made none at all. The lawyer resumed his argument, maintaining now that the plays could not have been written by a low-class man of no culture, and also that Lord Bacon must have studied his art in Germany, as proved by Hamlet's reference to Wittenberg. The others let him hold forth without contradiction, impressed perhaps by his fluent if horrible English. He was a flawless specimen of that German type altogether, for presently as a swan came gliding past it turned his thoughts to Lohengrin and he favoured the company with an aria in a confident but reedy tenor; and, as the launch turned for home in the soft light of early evening, with much pathos he recited the inevitable 'Über allen Gipfeln ist Ruh, in allen Wipfeln spürest Du kaum einen Hauch ... '

The temptation was irresistible.

'A charming lyric,' I observed at the conclusion. 'Did you know it was not in fact by Goethe?'

'*Not by Goethe*, now! Mees! Please!' From the outrage in his voice, it might have been supposed that I had baited him steadily throughout the trip.

'Cribbed, word for word, from a very ancient Greek poet,' I informed him happily. I owed this scrap of learning to a scholarly friend and if asked for the poet's name would have been in a fix; but he turned his back on me, as beneath contempt, and began talking about what he wanted for dinner.

Still, one man at least in Stratford-on-Avon was interested in Shakespeare, if only to demolish him.

The habits of the local bus service were a boon on this occasion, for had they been punctual I should have missed the coach to Worcester and been stuck in Stratford for the night. And I was doubly pleased to catch it, as the journey was enlivened by a girl who sat next to me, a warm blowsy expansive creature with a flow of uninhibited reminiscence. She was on holiday, had been travelling with a fellow but he walked out on her because she had borrowed some of his money without asking, funny how mean they often are. Stratford was not bad, but she was looking out for another bloke and had been disappointed: now she would have a go at Worcester before returning to Brum. Nothing steady, just for the time she was there, bed and meals and someone to talk to, she liked a bit of fun. Culture too, cathedrals and places, but you needed a fellow to enjoy them with. The one who walked out was always good for a laugh, pity he was so mean. She wasn't a gold-digger, nor a thief, but from the way he carried on ... This latterday Tearsheet kept it up almost without drawing breath, providing a wealth of social information and comment while the time slipped pleasantly by. She was the only person I had met that day who might have appealed to Shakespeare. I parted from her with regret, and gave her my address but she never came to see me. 'Hopefully', as she would have said, she had been suited and satisfied.

Chapter Sixteen

The great natural pleasure ground that this part of England is contains many others made by man. Two of them are the Westonbirt arboretum near Tetbury and the Wildfowl Trust at Slimbridge, both within easy reach of Gloucester. Or rather, they would be provided one was driven there by somebody able to read maps or with a sense of direction. The young friend who took me possessed neither qualification, but our day was all the richer for it, as her frequent detours brought us through beautiful villages and countryside that were not, so to speak, properly on the menu. In particular, we passed by great fields of rape in bloom, of a yellow so brilliant and, fine as the day was, the sun appeared to be pouring down only on that and the surrounding landscape looked dim as if overclouded.

Eventually we arrived. The little cluster of buildings, information centre, offices, refreshment room, was very simple in line, with a curious feel of Japan about it. Spring was one of the best times to see the place, the other of course being autumn, and we had chosen to go on a Saturday, but there were no crowds, no noise, litter or other signs of popular enjoyment. Groups of people strolled quietly through the woods, talking if at all in decent English undertones. A notice here and there reminded the public that nothing was to be picked or rooted up, and no doubt was necessary, for even the most civilized of gardeners are capable of dreadful deeds: otherwise, there seemed to be no rules at all, or any need for them.

There was a wonderful profusion of trees and shrubs, familiar and exotic, placed with careful art to show each other off. One great feature was the variety of rhododendron in the Savill Glade, fullgrown trees rather than shrubs, which flower from January to late June. Others, lovely too but smaller, grew beside cedar, cupressus and larch in the Loop Walk: the Acer

Glade had a collection of Japanese maple, including the Osa-kazuki which turns a fiery scarlet in October and which the people of Japan flock to admire with an almost religious fervour; and there was the Silk Wood, with our homely but exquisite bluebell carpeting the ground under the trees. It was a pity perhaps that name-plates, such as are usually found in parks, were not supplied, because only a specialist could know what many of the specimens were or where they came from: why these facts should increase the pleasure I cannot tell, but they do.

Days rather than hours were needed to explore this heavenly place as it deserved. And to wander about in wood-land is like walking beside the sea, inducing a tranquil frame of mind which takes no account of trivial matters, such as time. Presently, however, we recalled that we had yet to visit the Wildfowl Trust, with the probability of losing our way several times over first. Our plan of getting directions from the Information Officer came to nothing, as the cheerful young woman in charge, who knew the place well, had never started out from here; but fortunately the Trust stays open until the birds retire at dusk and we arrived in spite of ourselves in time to see a part at least of the huge collection of over three thousand, with 180 different kinds.

Where all at Westonbirt was peace and quiet, all here was bustle and brio. The mating season was in full swing, and many of the birds could only be described as sex mad. Drakes shot through the water after a duck like sharks pursuing a titbit, and such was the general billing and cooing, the amor-ous displays and dances, that really one felt quite out of it. Even family duties could not damp their ardour: we watched a moorhen collecting sticks, straws and feathers for the nest his mate was building inside their wooden home, handing them in at the door and setting out to look for others, until his roving eye lit on a female and whoosh! he was off in a flash, all else forgotten.

The flamingos, one of the star attractions, were a comic turn in themselves, standing about in groups and apparently deep in serious meditation, interrupted by sudden unbridled passes at each other and bouts of shameless necking. Those who grew weary of the sport would go a little way off, tuck

149

their head under a wing and one leg under the other and, a bundle of rosy feathers perched decoratively on a long thin stilt, remain motionless with Do Not Disturb written all over them. They were an entrancing sight under the blue sky and against the fresh early green of the bushes round their paddock.

Another draw was the Black Swan, whom we did not see but of whom a friend had told me an interesting story. Normally aloof and supercilious like most swans, at the very sight of her he had flown into a towering rage, hissing, beating his wings and trying to get at her through the protective wire. His keeper was unable to account for this behaviour but my friend, a woman keenly sensitive to the feelings of others, thought she understood it. She had been dressed entirely in black, but to be black was *his* prerogative, marking him out from the common herd and raising him above it; and his pride had rebelled against her effrontery. I am not sure of the scientific value of this view but, in the absence of any other, it seems worth consideration.

We did not make for anything in particular but walked about enjoying whatever we happened to see. Birds surely get more fun out of life, have more zest for it, than most of creation. Their lovely singing at dawn and dusk has no counterpart among animals, unless the lugubrious baying of the moon by dogs may be allowed as such. Nor do I know of any animals who actually disport themselves except the otter and the zany gnu of South Africa, while here gulls were joyously gliding on currents of air, swans taking off and landing with tremendous panache, moorhens busy with games of bob apple and follow-my-leader, baby ducks and geese exploring on their own while their parents doubtless canoodled elsewhere, all apparently on pleasure bent and without a care in the world. A diverting sight was a pair of blue-billed ducks who were toddling round in the wake of a solemn fellow wreathed with cameras of various sizes, studying his every move and passing remarks that sounded derisive in nature.

There was a great sense of freedom here: the care and thought behind it all were admirable, and one never felt that Slimbridge was a Zoo, a place of captivity. Apart from special

cases, like the tropical house where hummingbirds and tana-
gers live in warmth among the plants of their native jungle,
the birds are mostly unconfined, with plenty of space, wide
stretches of water, sandy beaches, streams, boskies, whatever is needed for their contentment. It was all superlatively
well done, and in the English way, as if no one had really
been trying: the experience of that afternoon was unforgett-
able.

Our original plan was to round the day off with a visit to
the Forest of Dean, one of the last Royal Forests left, but I
discarded it. A poignant memory had come to me of another
drive with young Clodagh, admittedly years ago, from Achill
Island in Mayo to Dublin. All she had to do was keep in a
straight line eastward, and one would have thought it foolproof, but there were psychological and mechanical factors
which I had not foreseen. She was to have picked me up at
'about' ten o'clock, which meant quarter to four: within
moments of starting off she ran over a neighbour's chicken;
and we had barely passed Foxford when smoke began to
pour from the engine. For a while she maintained that it was
only mist, as she was wearing dark glasses, but it continued
belching forth, growing blacker, until the jalopy came to a
halt. The fan-belt had gone and was pulled out, by a helpful
rustic, looking for all the world like a piece of bad knitting.

There followed one of the dramas so dear to the Irish heart,
with advice and counter-advice from those spectators that
always spring up as if from the ground, a make-shift towing
arrangement which broke down immediately, a trudge to the
nearest garage for qualified assistance, a long wait while
repairs were done, then off again, stopping once for a horrible meal which only near-starvation could have induced me
to eat and finally limping into Dublin as the cocks began to
crow.

Clodagh had been a medical student then and now was a
competent dermatologist, and it was base of my memory to
bring all that up: nevertheless, having tasted her powers if
only once I was loth to see them brought into play again.
And curious adventures had befallen us that very day, one of
them worthy of Don Quijote himself. She had spotted a
massive building far off on the horizon beyond my range of

vision, and the noble outline of it persuaded her that this was an ancient castle, with towers, moat, keeps and other romantic features, and I agreed to yet another 'little detour'. It had proved to be a gasworks. With this in mind, and fearing that even if we got to the forest we might lose ourselves in it and never get out, I took charge, insisted that she followed the estuary and then the Wye valley as far as Ross, after which it was a straight run home.

Apart from the hazards involved it would not have been seemly to dash round the forest like Americans ticking an item off their schedule. It is an area of great richness, historical and natural, to be explored at leisure and also to read about in a copious literature. Enclosed by the rivers Severn and Wye, it has a character all its own and the inhabitants have a remarkable sense of their difference from ordinary people.

In Norman times it was a hunting ground for kings and their privileged guests, which explains the scanty reference in the Domesday Book, this being compiled for tax purposes and royal chases being exempt. Under the Tudors, that changed and it became an essential source of timber for the growing Navy, having to contend with the inroads made upon supplies by the iron ore industry and their furnaces. Then Charles I, in his frantic efforts to raise money on the side, took to granting leases for large sums and finally sold the entire forest to Sir John Wintour for £106,000: it was a misguided act, as the natives were so furious at Sir John's programme of enclosure and felling that they withheld their support from the Royalist cause in the Civil War. They were little better off under the Protectorate, however, as heavy cutting of timber went on without reafforestation and all the iron works were demolished: in fact, no matter who possessed the region at any time, the people always seemed to cop it. Under the Restoration all kinds of plans were considered and changes brought about, one being the rise and development of the coalmining industry which continued steadily to our present day, until nationalisation ruined the small inefficient collieries and the Forest became a depressed area. The story of this beautiful part of England is a long one of friction between opposing interests and of suffering by helpless people caught up in them.

There is a vivid and moving account of a coal-miner's family life during the hard times, written by Winifred Foley and called *A Child in the Forest*. It tells of hardship, or actual hunger even, with a self-denying father, indomitable harassed mother, the squabbles, disasters, the rare tiny treats that came like a fall of manna, and the chronic insecurity they bore with only their pride to sustain them. That pride was simply in what they were, mining people of the Dean, and quite unaffected by externals. There was a revealing episode when the mother, who was strict with the children at home, coolly took them 'scrumping', that is, robbing an apple orchard, and they were routed by an angry farmer. There was no shame in this, no dent in their self-esteem, merely disappointment over the apples, to which they half imagined they had a right. The book was well received, deservedly for the writing, but also perhaps because the middle classes have developed a taste for reading about low life where once they hungered for news of the aristocracy; and the photograph of the author, smartly dressed and self-assured, seemed like the ending of a modern fairy tale, with the heroine raised to suburbia.

Now it is no longer a royal preserve, a centre of mines or quarries or a depressed area but a rural amenity, with all that this includes of good and bad. There are inns, caravan and camping sites, picnic places, and signposts galore, some of which inform you when you are in a beautiful, or 'scenic', part in case you should fail to notice it yourself. With unconscious humour the Forestry Commission Guide has even a photograph of a girl described as a Pathfinder, studying a map beside one of these whose arms point to waymarked forest paths in every direction. The pleasures of exploration, losing yourself, wondering where you will end up and what you will find on the way are evidently out of date in our ordered existence. But there are magnificent stretches of woodland, oak predominating as in olden times, their insect life feeding a host of birds, many familiar, others rare, and ponds, streams, waterfalls, sudden views of glorious countryside through a clearing in the trees or a rise in the land.

At this time the earlier spring flowers were done and the

later had not appeared, but throughout the summer, says the Guide, there would be a profusion of them, those that love marsh and shade and those that flourish in sandy, rocky or leafy soil and sun. No doubt many that are disappearing outside under the ruthless methods of modern farming will have found a sanctuary here; and people who are fond of wild creatures and have time and patience to watch them will be rewarded by a tremendous range, from Pigmy Shrew and Whiskered Bat to fallow deer, last remnants of the original species that roamed the Forest in Norman times.

I spent but a day in this delectable spot and would gladly have spent a week or more, preferably on my own. This implies no criticism of the American friends who took me, cheerfully driving whichever way I asked them to and for-bearing to remark that the Forest was peanuts to what they had back home; it was just that, like so many of their compat-riots, they had either lost the use of their legs or never had it, and the Dean should really be explored on foot. As, in fact, should every other place of beauty and interest.

Chapter Seventeen

I now had an amusing and happy interlude which, like so many good experiences, came out of the blue. While staying at the Stanbrook guest-house earlier on I had met Mary Rennell of Rodd, a well-known character there and in other communities up and down the country: indeed, much of her time was spent in driving from one to the next, as she was fascinated by the monastic life and those who followed it. This was notable in itself, because she came of stock that might have been expected to frown on Holy Church, her grandfather being an Earl of Antrim. Much of her childhood in World War I had been spent in the family home, where Catholicism would have been a matter for the servants' hall; nevertheless, late in life she became a convert, though with none of the dreadful zeal that is associated with the species. She had warm humanity and a bewitching sense of fun, was an accomplished artist and a woman of wide culture.

We shared a table at meal-times and I took to her at once, relishing the many facets of her personality as they appeared one after the other in the course of a single meal. One day, I remember, that of the *grande dame* made a rare and brief appearance: we were chatting comfortably after breakfast when an officious oblate asked us to go as the manageress wanted to clear away. Mary smiled at her vaguely and went on talking as if she had not heard, and the oblate retired in confusion.

I was delighted, then, on revisiting the monastery to find her there but sorry to learn the reason for it. Her cook was to go into hospital almost at once for an operation. This came at a most unfortunate time, as Mary was about to hold an exhibition of paintings in her private gallery and there was much to do, but she made light of that, her thoughts all being for the cook. I love cooking and on the spur of the moment offered to

155

come and do hers; she accepted with alacrity, and that same afternoon the pair of us were on our way to the Rodd in a car that she drove with true Anglo-Irish elan.

Mary had snow-white hair, pink cheeks and eyes the colour of the sea, and was elegantly bohemian in her dress. She needed supports in walking on the flat and a special hoist to get her upstairs, but she was so lively that one never thought of her as disabled and so young in mind that one never thought of her age. Her chief companion now was a tiny poodle who bounced about like a ball of angora or lay curled up with only her tongue protruding to show which end was which. She was an awkward little customer with a habit of flying at strangers who came into her room or, once there, got up from their seat, and snapping at their ankles. She never bit me, however, for her principal targets were men and it was fun to watch the nervous crablike gait of Alf the handyman and the gardener when they knew she was at large. Signs of fear brought out the demon in her and the sight of that shrinking pair transformed her into a shrieking fury. But as time passed, especially when Mary was on safari and I had the sole care of her, she relaxed and we ended up good friends. Intelligent and pleasure-loving as poodles usually are, she only wanted amusement, affection and company.

The Rodd was a delightful building altogether, standing a short distance from Presteigne it was no stately home but a roomy old manor farmhouse which had been in the family for a very long time, gone out once as a dowry and later bought back. Life in the winter there might be rugged, with the powerful draughts – 'Tudor draughts,' Mary called them – moaning along the passages; windows rattled, stairs creaked and floors were uneven, which was disconcerting until one got to know them. But I fell in love with it directly. The drawing-room had been the wainers' barn, the massive beams were still overhead and the original woodwork still showed in the walls, but it was so attractively furnished and comfortably heated that one had the best of both worlds. It was pleasant too to have space all round and height above in this age of box-sized flats and low ceilings, and to sleep in an English fourposter bed even without curtains.

156

My bedroom was altogether noble, of the kind that used to go with apparel laid out, washing collected and quietly returned and early morning tea in a silver pot, brought by a maid with streamers in her cap, but these had gone the way of butlers, chauffeurs and similar frills. In fact, I had to make my own bed, but this may have been because on arriving I had introduced myself to the kitchen as 'the cook' and a sturdy refusal to wait on fellow servants has been common to English staff in every age. The plumbing was on the Tudor side, but there were majestic water-closets with broad wooden seats like a church pew, the downstairs 'gentleman's' one of special charm with a notice purloined from the House of Lords insisting that 'Members will adjust their robes before they leave'.

I set about my duties with a will, enjoying the big kitchen, the abundant *batterie de cuisine* and the absence of modern gadgets. It was a treat to cook for Mary, a valiant trencherman without any fads and very quick to praise. One instance of this touched me greatly, as showing how modest and uncomplaining she was: I always laid the breakfast table with small forks and put out clean napkins at every meal, thinking of both as natural and being entirely of that gentleman's mind who had heard of napkin rings but never wished to see one; and Mary said 'how *nice* to have small forks again and no grubby linen', as if she could not have simply given orders about it.

It was not long before my activities were extended to wider fields. The gentle Lady Rennell shared with the autocratic Mrs Knox of Somerville and Ross a gift for divining the different kinds of work her people might be able for and setting them to it. Although I could not myself draw a recognizable pig, I was an artist's daughter and had many artist friends, so that something of them perhaps had rubbed off on me; and very soon I was hanging pictures and pricing them to the manner born and having a great deal of fun.

The gallery was an old black and white cottage, built on a cruck, just two minutes' walk from the Manor Farm down a path with fine poppies, peonies and roses, together with luxuriant docks and other weeds. It must be said that the stark white walls with their heavy beams straggling slantwise

157

across them were not an ideal background for paintings of delicate colour; and there was a further drawback in the matter of security, provided by a single massive old key which sometimes turned in the front door lock and sometimes did not.

The point was raised in a telephone call from the artist's son, who said the insurance company was asking for details. I went to see Mary about it, and found her resting after a little commotion about her oblate's Benedictine medal. She feared that it had been inadvertently flushed down the w.c. but it proved to have got stuck in her shawl. I listed the questions that the insurance agent had put, and had to tell her how unlikely it was that he would be content with her replies.

'Well then,' her ladyship said, after further thought and somewhat surprisingly, 'tell him to go and bugger himself!' With that she burst into a wild glorious laugh, which she also had in common with Mrs Knox, and in which I helplessly joined. When I had recovered a little, I returned to the telephone to assure the caller that the matter was receiving our best attention.

Some time afterwards Mary told me she had felt it necessary to speak of this lapse in Confession, and that her confessor had laughed nearly as much as I.

The show was quite a real success, considering that the gallery lay *perdu* in the depths of Powys country. Friends and neighbours attended the vernissage, turning it into an extremely enjoyable party. There was an Irish doctor who was the brother of a boon companion of mine in Dublin days, one of a large family said to be melancholic but socially each as amusing as the next. About the best, and by far the most expensive, picture was bought very soon after the guests arrived, which was good for morale; and on subsequent days there was a constant trickle of visitors, pleasant, cultivated people from here and there who talked knowledgeably about art and literature and foreign lands; but the one who made a lasting impression on me was of a different kind altogether.

It was a youth in shabby denims with black frizzy hair, silver earrings and a pencil behind one ear, who came slouching in with a sullen defiant class-conscious look as if expecting to be despised. I feared he might have thoughts of

158

raiding the till and, to distract his thoughts from this, asked if he were an artist himself. Instantly and utterly transformed, he told me that he was, but that, working as a carpenter on building sites in the day, he was too tired to do very much at night. Once a week he went to the evening School of Art in Leominster.

We went round the pictures together and he made comments that were very much to the point. There was one of a dressmaker's dummy, half swathed, half bare, and I remarked that, excellent as it was in itself, I should not want to see a dressmaker's dummy every day on my wall. But the boy smiled indulgently and began to discuss it purely in terms of line, colour, perspective and light. He was wholly an artist, wholly visual. And he spoke of his own painting as well, what he was trying and hoping to do, how he always made his own frames, how cheap ready-made ones could ruin a good work. It was one of the most interesting talks I ever had with a working man and I wished I could see his pictures, and also that some of the public money lavished on gimmicky arrangers of bricks and old tins might have been diverted to his use.

In the evening or at the weekends Mary took me for enchanting drives through Shropshire and Radnor, now called something else after that misguided mix-up but I forget what. To call these counties 'unspoiled' gives no idea of their wild beauty and emptiness; large parts of Radnor in particular seem almost uninhabited. The landscape is immensely varied, coniferous plantations covering entire hills, mountain meadows dotted with cattle and sheep and a single majestic oak or elm rising above them, streams rushing and tumbling through deep valleys, now and then the gaunt sheer cliff of a quarry then moorland again with many kinds of different birds. When we crossed the border into Wales, it was odd how dramatically the architecture changed, the villages angular and stony in contrast to the snug mellow ones of England, just a very few miles away.

The curving lanes of the country were narrow, too narrow for vehicles to pass, so that if two vehicles met one of them had to back until it reached one of the widened spaces. The hedges on either side were too tall to see what might be

159

coming, a source of many hazards. Mary was an impetuous driver, too, trusting largely to her horn to clear the way ahead but with a knack of pulling up short a couple of inches from the oncoming car, which proved invaluable time and again.

While exceedingly quick and shrewd in many ways, she could be somewhat vague in others. There was a memorable Polish Evening in honour of the Pope and his literary works which we were to attend after dining at a cottage tucked away in a remote valley. Instructions on how to get there had been given but Mary had failed to master them: we got to the crossroads mentioned but took a wrong turning there and ended up at a large farmhouse, deserted except for two chained and howling dogs. The back door had been left open, a broom leaned against the wall (upside down, a hint in some parts that the man of the house is away and company welcome) and a woman's bedroom slipper lay on the kitchen flags inside.

'This will be it,' Mary decided. 'I know she has two dogs!'

But hardly two such miserable curs, I thought, and the house itself with the hideous china urns holding seedy plants and the dire 'suites' of furniture did not quite fit in with our hostess to be as she had been described to me. But Mary was unaffected by this or perhaps she thought all middle-class interiors looked alike and, relying on the evidence of the dogs she urged me to knock again.

The curs howled more dismally than ever but nobody came. At last we drove back to the crossroads and started afresh. A drawback of lovely unspoiled country is that there is never a soul, not even a man behind a hedge, to point out the way. This time however our hit or miss method was successful and we arrived, horribly late but not more so than a priest who followed soon after. He was dressed in a fine suit of clothes that sat awkwardly on his peasant frame and, seemingly unconscious of the hour, greeted us all in a broad Sligo accent.

Our hostess was of charming appearance and manner, and so true to arty type that I could gladly have embalmed her. She had regular features and wide clear eyes, and her hair was bobbed and fringed like that of a mediaeval page; and she was dressed in exotic foreign style, dirndl and stepjanke, as if trying to escape from her irremediable Englishness.

Having been told that she was a Quaker I was somewhat anxious about our entertainment, for a non-alcoholic Polish evening hardly bore thinking about; but she immediately plied us with drink, warning us to make haste as time was short. I amused myself wondering what we should have to eat, either pizza or quiche Lorraine I would have betted, as these two dishes invariably go with ethnic attire. As a matter of fact we had both, with a delicious salad and an excellent glass of hock: the pudding had to be skipped because of our unpunctuality, but it would have been mousse for a fiver. The priest said grace in his heavy brogue, urging us in the fashionable charismatic style to partake of all the good things with enjoyment while not forgetting the people all round the world who were deprived of them. If our hostess wished us all at the bottom of the sea after the trouble she had taken on our behalf, she gave no sign of it and was as sweet as if we had been dead on time and bringing champagne.

The Polish evening surpassed my apprehensions. It was held in what had been a little country church with the carved wooden ceiling typical of the Welsh border and now was a meeting-place or Centre. A number of solemn young men stood about the entrance with lighted candles in their hands and one of these escorted us to our chairs. They were right in the middle of the front row, so we could not allow our attention to wander, and on each of them was a new candle with a cardboard frill to catch the grease. Uneasy memories of processions in Poland ran through my mind. A large wrought-iron cross, looking like a contemporary set of fire-irons hung from the roof with a posy of flowers tied to its foot but no figure on it; possibly it had been thought that a real crucifix might offend some of the audience.

The proceedings were as long drawn out as things Slavonic are apt to be. First of all a handsome professor, with a mane of silvery hair and the features of a refined Beethoven, spoke to us of the Pope, whom he had known as Cardinal Wojtyla of Cracow, before reading a long series of his poems in Polish. Very few of those present could understand a word. After that, a man from the BBC read the translations, and

161

read them very nicely too, but either they were poor in themselves or, as I suspect, deep spiritual thoughts do not necessarily make for good poetry.

As if that were not trying enough, we next had to stand up, light our candles and wave them aloft. This was supposed to be in affirmation of something or other, and I wondered if the English element felt half as foolish as it looked. Still with our flaming dripping candles on high, we then recited the Paternoster and the Credo, and how typical it was of today that while we no longer kneel for 'et homo factus est' or cross ourselves at 'The resurrection of the dead' we should be asked to make this silly empty gesture.

At long last it was over, and the solemn young men could start chirping about the great success it had been and how splendid the turn-out. Mary submitted to being the lioness of the occasion with charming grace, her own parish priest, a German who licked his thumb before turning a page, being particularly attentive. The BBC man told me that he had once acted in a radio play of mine, but I could not remember it and anyhow was feeling as prickly as a hedgehog.

This delightful stretch of countryside must be a hotbed of such happenings and of the way-out and trendy altogether. On the feast of St Peter and St Paul Mary took me to a church in Weombry, tipping me off beforehand that the incumbent was rather 'bouncy'. I think she was alluding to a spiritual quality, but he was so short and tubby, it would have come as no surprise if he had bounced up the aisle like a rubber ball. As so often with such priests, his vestments appeared to have been designed by himself; of this I cannot be sure, but I would have betted that it had been 'worked' for him by some local lady. He had the round head of a bulldog and the short little nose that betokens both pugnacity and self-approval; and, as if the new English mass had not four dreadful versions to choose from, he did a certain amount of improvisation without improving matters at all.

There was the usual business of bringing females into the picture as much as possible. The harmonium was played by a girl, dressed in shabby denim pants and an Indian muslin blouse, who first removed her slippers to reveal her large bare feet. No doubt this gave a better purchase on the pedals, but it made a curious impression. The readings and responsorial psalm were given out by a woman too, wearing a mannish peaked cloth cap and a scarlet trouser suit that was injudicious for one of her ample build. She kept a hand in her pocket all the way through and stood with one knee bent like a weary old cab horse.

The sign of peace, that bugbear of right-thinking persons, was initiated by the priest kissing the harmonium girl and shaking hands with his acolyte: these then proceeded down the aisle, bowing, gesticulating and otherwise manifesting goodwill to the congregation. A ritual odder than any yet took place when we came to what used to be called the Elevation: the priest, the two women and the acolyte all held a saucer-like object with the wafer upon it, as mediums do at a seance, while the priest intoned a rubric of his own devising. Only consideration for Mary stopped me from hurling a peseta into the collection basket when it came round.

She of course took it all with calm toleration and even asked the wretch to supper; but luckily he had a previous date, as he called it. The village of Weombry was attractive at least and very much en fête this evening, gay with bunting and streamers, the children pelting along in go-cart races and a lively stir and bustle in every narrow lane. The drive here from the Rodd had been enchanting and was equally so going back, the country wearing a new face when seen from another direction, so that it was two drives rather than one.

That was our last outing together, as a real stand-in for the ailing cook was now available and shortly due to arrive. On my last evening Mary said she would like to give me one of her drawings as a keepsake, the portrait of a Carmelite Mother Superior whom we had visited and to whom I had been very much drawn. The shabby little parlour in which she received us had seemed as if lit up the moment she entered it; and the warmth of her manner, the immediate way she took people into her friendship, the merry common sense of all she said, had put me in mind of another Carmelite, the ever fascinating and lovable Teresa de Jesús.

What then was my inward dismay when Mary, with quiet pride, handed me a lithograph which depicted a formidable unsmiling woman, apparently about to rebuke an erring novice; and my further bewilderment, as she explained that her special gift was to look through the outer semblance to the real person behind. This rather hinted at baffling depths in Mary's own character, so much so that I could not resist, later on, asking Mother Prioress of Stanbrook how the portrait Mary did of herself had struck her. 'As satanic' was the laughing reply.

The lithograph was beautifully done, and numbered too, as with some limited edition de luxe; it was clear that the artist prized it highly and was marking her approval of my services by the presentation. I accepted it in that spirit, and the whole affair but increased her charm in my eyes, for there should always be something to marvel at in our friends. I hoped the incoming cook would know about forks and napkins and also the kind of food that Mary enjoyed, since if not nothing would ever be said. My time in her house had been of the happiest and most diverting, and remains a delightful memory to this day.

Chapter Eighteen

Travelling about the country here, so often called the heart of
England, I came to think of it as such, a heart that pounded
away calmly and steadily. Nothing seems to shock or worry it,
you could not imagine it missing a beat. It was a warm heart
too, full of neighbourly concern and good works that went
past the neighbour and embraced the globe. Not only our
native spastics, aged poor and mentally handicapped were to
benefit from all the jumble sales, coffee mornings,
bring-and-buys and fêtes, but the Boat People, the famished
Somalis, the down-and-outs of Calcutta or the victims of any
natural disaster in any part of the world. An earthquake in
some far-off land would be followed by sponsored feats of
endurance from jogging to pushing a bedstead along for
miles, and stickers in motor-cars would appeal for blankets or
blood. At the same time there was no lively interest in foreign
places or particular fondness for aliens of any description: it
seemed more as if some vestigial spirit of Empire made
English people feel vaguely responsible for everyone everywhere.

I have a tenderness for village fêtes and their varied attractions, from three-legged races for adults ('Come on, ladies and
gents, don't let the kids beat you!') to Madame Esther in her
spangled booth who tells such improbable fortunes. The siz-
zling corpse of a pig revolves on a spit before a blazing fire
with a strong man to carve it, a tub of apple sauce and a pile of
baps near by: the fare is sturdy rather than elegant, but you
pay your money like a sportsman and somehow manage to
swallow it. Another live pig is to be bowled for, or his weight
may be guessed, or he is put up in a raffle, with a keen-witted
buyer there to take him off your hands if you win. A brass
band, usually of boys from a local school with short hair and
tidy suits, will play a medley from Sousa, Offenbach or Gilbert

and Sullivan, and Scouts, Guides and Cubs display their
fitness while an École de Danse from town performs a familiar routine, culminating in that solo by a four-year-old who
breaks down in the middle and runs weeping to her mother.
There is sure to be an impressive piece of obsolete machinery, a nineteenth-century steam-roller or fire engine, all
polished up and lent by Colonel Someone. Inside the hall, a
matron with County written all over her is weaving a basket
or spinning cloth or demonstrating some other archaic skill;
and there are stalls of produce, craft and art, ranging from
home-made cake and jam to knitted gloves, poker-work and
a watercolour perhaps, of the local bridge or a Small Brown
Owl. That splendid body, the Women's Institute, has provided a tea of cucumber sandwiches, featherlight scones and
pastries for next to nothing: Mrs Collingham has tastefully
arranged the floral decoration, as she has done these twenty
odd years: indeed, all the ladies who have worked so hard
are to be complimented on the afternoon's success; and the
local correspondent of the Echo, Clarion or Gazette
feverishly writes down their names, lest by an unhappy
omission his own should be mud. Everybody takes part in
everything and in due course a substantial sum goes off to
another deserving cause.

It need hardly be said that this loving-kindness extends to
the animal world, perhaps even in greater measure. If anything could shake the people out of their placid good
humour, it might be cruelty to or neglect of a dumb friend.
This is a supposition on my part because I never heard of any
such thing in my travels hereabouts, and indeed the prevailing attitude occasionally seemed rather extravagant even to
me, an animal lover myself. In a little hamlet, for example, I
once found a poster announcing a special service for pets in
the parish church at which all God's creatures would be
welcome; and I wondered what the Rector would say if some
one turned up with a crocodile and a kangaroo. For that
matter, what would he have done if, taking him at his word,
the owners had brought their pets and then made off, promising to collect them when the service was over, like children
from a party? Would he have preached with fervour to them,
as St Francis did to the birds? Or would he, in the good old

English way, have composedly read the prayers and lessons and given out the hymns as if nothing strange were afoot? If so, I should have very much liked to be there. But unless one knew the Rector, of course, one could not be sure if this were eccentricity of the endearing kind that once flourished in England or sentimentality of the *Du côté de chez Winnie le Pooh* description that one would gladly dispense with.

I am more at home with the matter-of-fact approach of the country people, who accept animals for what they are and Nature herself for what she is. You don't find them shuddering at the thought of a slaughterhouse in the village, because they know there must be slaughterhouses if we are to have any meat. How the dainty folk who sign petitions and protests against these buildings imagine the joints and chops get on to their tables, I cannot think: they always put me in mind of those Russian aristocrats in Nabokov's *Speak, Memory* who would go a-mushrooming in the forest for fun, hand the baskets over to servants on their return and meet the mushrooms later in a delicious cream sauce, without an idea in the world of what had happened in between.

In one of the villages I visited, never mind which, I met a delightful character who was as down to earth as could be. I was in the local pub, and the talk happened to turn on foxes and their new habit of moving into towns and cities, rather like the rural population itself. I put some question about foxy ways, and the company told me I had better have a word with George. He would be in presently, and he knew all about them.

'Is he a huntsman?' I asked.

This innocent question provoked a roar of merriment.

'You could call him one,' the landlord said. 'But he calls himself a handyman.'

More laughter followed and then, as if on cue, in came George, a short wiry man with keen blue eyes and the hesitant gait of one who is frequently ambushed.

'Lady asking about foxes, George,' the landlord said.

'Ah,' said George, pensively watching while his pint was drawn. Then he took a pull at it, studying me over the edge of the mug, apparently wondering if I were a fit person to entrust with information. 'Foxes, eh. Long subject, that.'

167

'Is it true they shack up with badgers?'

'They do,' said George. 'Well no, not reely shack up. The badgers don't fancy the fox's scent, though they're a musty high-smelling lot theirselves. They allow the foxes in the sett and block up the passages between 'em, like Big House people shutting off the servants' hall.'

There was renewed laughter at this, George evidently being a wag as well as a handyman.

'Would you like to see one, miss?' he asked. 'You're welcome to come along if so. I'm on my way to the wood, happens.'

Another mystifying outbreak from the company.

I was glad of the invitation and we went off together. As long as we were within the village, George chatted amiably on general topics, weather, crops, the lateness of everything, changes since he was a boy, dearth of partridges and its cause, a matter he dwelt on with some acrimony. When we got to the wood, he abruptly fell silent and looked about him, noting all he saw as if each newly broken twig or unfamiliar heap of feathers held some message for him.

'That's the sett over there,' he said presently, pointing. 'We won't go nearer, there's a vixen in whelp behind. See all that stuff lying about? That's the badgers' bedding, put out to air. Very partikkler, are badgers.'

'Shall we see one?'

'No fear. They've heard us.'

We were standing beside a pool, evidently a communal drinking-place, as the soft edges had a maze of little footprints which George now carefully examined.

'Ah then, she's whelped,' he said triumphantly. 'See her pug marks there, and the other ones beside 'em? They're lighter. The cubs are out.'

He left me after this, having further business in the wood, and I went back to the village, thinking him better than Sherlock Holmes. Indeed, so impressed was I with his deduction and general grasp of woodland life, that I spoke of it to a man I met that evening, who owned these woods and some of the fields beside them. To my surprise, he gave a shout of laughter worthy of the assembled public in the local.

'George the handyman!' he chortled. 'That's our number

one poacher. Yes, he knows his way round, blast him. But what can be done? I don't really preserve these days, my old keeper's retiring soon and the young men aren't any good.'

I suddenly had what might perhaps, without vainglory, be called a moment of inspiration. 'Why not offer the keeper's place to George?' I said.

He looked at me for a while in amazement, and then thoughtfully replied, 'I might do worse than that.'

There was endless pleasure in roaming about the country-side at this time of year, taking one way or the other, giving the car her bonnet, so to speak, since with everything so beautiful there was no need to look for routes beforehand. A car there has to be, for the rare buses keep to the main roads, and how the inhabitants of some little rural hamlets move about is hard to imagine. The young manage by stopping other people's cars and demanding to be ferried for nothing. It is their normal means of travel and they would not dream of taking a bus or a train even if such were provided. Things go wrong occasionally, girls may be raped, but this no more puts them off than the possibility of a crash could prevent us from going by air. But how do their elders travel? Perhaps they do not, but snuggle down at home and look to the tele for news of the outside world. Even by the relaxed standards of the day the posts are odd, for a letter can take days to cover a mere thirty miles or so, having no doubt wended its way to a sorting office in Worcester, Hereford or Gloucester and then doubled back to its destination. There is something agreeably nonchalant in the attitude to mail hereabouts, reminding one of rural Spain where a telegram announcing the day and hour of one's arrival is often brought by a lad on a mule a week or so after one has left.

All this was in the outback, you might almost say the bush: nearer civilisation, between Upton on Severn and Malvern were two villages that I came to know very well, Hanley Swan and Hanley Castle. Each of them was quietly con-vinced of its superiority to the neighbour, a feeling common to every English village I ever knew.

There were certain points in the Castle's favour, one that it was all but free of caravan people and trippers, whereas the Swan had three large camping sites, a Holiday Centre for poor Birmingham children and a remand home up the road at Welland. As regards the holiday-makers, one would not begrudge them a taste of quiet countryside beauty if only they did not destroy it. Wherever they go with their loud voices, uncouth habits and the rubbish they scatter, they act as a mobile slum and, far from taking a share in the village, bestow a share of Birmingham on it. But poor things, it may be objected, they only stay a fortnight or so. That is true, but when their time is up, they are replaced by others exactly like them, wave after grisly wave throughout the season.

And then Hanley Castle is near the river, which adds life and interest to the place, as rivers always do. The Castle vanished a long time ago, but villages named for some stronghold long since gone are common in Worcestershire, and traces of the moat can still be seen, as a local patriot took care to inform me. A vivid account of it, however, exists in *Hanley Castle* by the Reverend A. Symonds. The book is subtitled 'The Chronicle of Richard Plantagenet Forrester', who was born there in 1622 when nearby Malvern Chase, now all tidy and suburban, was 'the home of the wild boar, the stag, the hare and the coney, while birds and squirrels found shelter in the great trees and masses of foliage which stretched away for miles'. It was Crown land and in 1632 a deforestation was begun to swell the ever-famished royal coffers until serious rioting broke out, not by nature-lovers but by squatters – someone should write a book on Squatting Through the Ages, as there is nothing new about it – and King Charles settled things by taking only a third and leaving the rest to local parishes. 'Some of the Squatters then became Royalist,' the author adds drily.

Young Forrester was of a Royalist family anyhow, and the Chronicle is mainly concerned with the part it played in the Civil War. The fascinating thing about the book is that it is an imaginative reconstruction, one might almost say an historical novel of rare accuracy, not by a contemporary author but by one of those Victorian parsons who steeped themselves in the lore of their parishes and the surrounding country. A portrait of him, calm, bearded, reflective, yet with something of the perennial boy there as well, faces the dedication to his 'good wife and true these forty years'. Perhaps it is impious to say that a man in Holy Orders 'ought' to have been anything else, in this case a novelist, but it is extraordinary how this learned divine could enter so fully into the life of a young officer of twenty or so, his life, loves, battles, his triumphs and disappointments. Only now and then does an incongruous note creep in, with some scholarly allusion to Shakespeare which would hardly have sprung from Richard's brain, or this comment on a Rector of that time: 'Poor old man, he lived long enough to find the use of his loved Prayer Book made penal, and the highest of our Church Festivals abolished,' something which, one feels, would have worried the hero not at all.

For the most part, however, it is an enthralling account of the Civil War with its special horrors, bitterness and enmity between lifelong friends and neighbours, bloody battles waged over the countryside where they were born and reared, and the uncertainty as to whom they could trust, who might secretly be against them, even as happened to Richard, suspicion of a faithful old family servant. Ludicrous atrocity stories went round, one that the Royalists were hunting and eating children: this arose from a single Royalist officer being presented with a whole young pig and being seen to carry it off wrapped in a cloak, after which Cromwellian children were kept indoors for miles around. The brutal greedy German troops brought over by Prince Rupert were faithfully dealt with, especially a General with the unattractive and compromising name of von Prig; equally so were the dismal Puritans with their hatred of beauty and grace in worship and of harmless enjoyment in ordinary life: they even managed to connect the traditional Christmas revels, the boar's head, wassail bowl, holly, mistletoe and Yule log with the powers of darkness below. In short, the book may be described as a rattling good read, and it is pleasant to imagine the benevolent old parson hard at work upon it in his quiet study, surrounded by tomes of a more learned and improving nature.

Hanley Castle has an interesting and beautiful mediaeval church, which is another one up on the Swan; and another feather in its cap is that the local bigwigs, the Lechmere family, live on in their house at Severn End to this day, while the Hornyolds of Blackmore Park at the Swan have long departed, their grounds a teeming caravan site. All country people love what they call the 'old' families, those that acquire a great deal of property and have the ability, craft or grit to hang on to it though the centuries. At least, that is what I take them to be, as in any other sense no family is older than the next, and in this region especially the same humble names crop up repeatedly in the local records, without anyone describing them as old. The Lechmeres qualify in the fullest degree, having lived in their ancient house since the Conquest. From Pamela Hurd's lively and informative guide book I learned that *Lech* is the old Breton word for love, while *mere* of course is the French for mother, and the pelicans in the family crest symbolize the mother-love of that bird, wounding her breast to feed her young on the blood. The house had passed through many adventures and vicissitudes in the course of time and has been much restored and added to; and it cannot be reckoned a thing of beauty. Except on rare and special occasions it is not open to the public as, odd though it may seem in this intrusive age, the owners like their privacy. The local people do not resent their aloofness, for an 'old' family has a right to be odd and the less you know about it, the more freely it can be discussed. There is no direct heir to the baronetcy now, and it will descend with the property itself to a most agreeable and knowledgeable bookseller in Malvern.

Hanley Swan took my fancy the moment I first set eyes on it, despite its regrettable links with the outside world. The village had a splendid green, broad and smooth with one giant oak, a noble tree of perfect shape, right in the middle, a pond covered with yellow and white nenuphars and merry with water-fowl of various kinds. To one side there was a fringe of trees with baby squirrels at their mad little games, leaping from bough to bough with the utmost nonchalance, and to the other, the long low white building of the Swan public house. All round about in the lanes leading off from this were old timbered farmhouses, large and small, washed pink, blue or white, with carefully tended flower gardens, some with bee hives at one end. It was early morning when I first arrived, and a delicious smell of bread, good honest bread, was coming from the village bakery; I had almost forgotten what fresh warm bread could smell like, and sniffed the air with rapture. Rooks were cawing and croaking importantly in such of the elms as had escaped the blight, and along the bridle paths beneath them strings of horsemen or children on ponies trotted briskly, drawing aside to let pedestrians pass with a polite 'Good morning!' And a little way up the road to Malvern, at St Gabriel's church with its tall slender spire, a group of ringers were practising on the bells, a lovely sound I had not heard for many a year. I met the Vicar coming away in a hurry, as if one could have enough of anything: he was a portly bearded gentleman who gave me a friendly smile. Later on I discovered he was a man of literary tastes, whose Notes in the parish magazine on the life of bee and bat and other rural topics were quite in the good old Anglican tradition.

It was a happy introduction to a place where apparently everything was just as it should be. Nevertheless, as I returned again and again and got to know the people, I found some of those born and bred there apt to shake their heads and declare that it was no longer a village at all.

'The Midland taint!' said one of them darkly. 'Commuters, settlers, foreigners . . . '

The absence of foreigners had struck me as one of its principal charms: indeed, there was only one to my knowledge, a gallant Polish airman who had fought with us in the war and must have been welcome anywhere. And, in fact, it was not he whom the speaker had in mind. He meant *foreigners*, moneyed people from towns who lived along a stretch of the Upton Road derisively named Millionaires' Row, or caravanners from Birmingham, the men obese and bearded, the women with their hair screwed up in curlers, and all with deplorable accents. Others too used the word *foreigners* in a sense peculiar to themselves. For all its beauty, the village green did have a crossroads running beside it where terrible accidents happened, resulting in deaths and grave injuries, after one of which a petition was drawn up asking the Council to take some action. A local man refused on the grounds that only foreigners were affected and, as one of the victims had been Asian, it looked as if racism were

173

rearing its ugly head; but not a bit of it, he merely meant travellers from Tewkesbury, Gloucester, Cheltenham and other outlying regions.

'Call that a pond, do you?' another man asked. I certainly did, especially on a fine sunny day as that was, with the white walls of the Swan and the little puffs of cloud overhead mirrored in its calm surface. Two families had just hatched out, one of fluffy little brown and yellow ducklings, who paddled demurely in Indian file behind their parents, and one of moorhen, small black imps bobbing about in the water, head down, rump in the air, expert divers already. But the malcontent eyed it sourly. 'You should have seen it before those youngsters cleaned it out. Volunteers, they were, from a University. It has never been the same since – why, it's hardly more than a puddle. Dug all the clay from the bottom, they did, wouldn't be told, of course, knew everything better.'

Others recalled with nostalgia the days when the Family, that is to say the Hornyolds, were the power in the land. The village green had belonged to them and they allowed the people to enjoy themselves there, with bonfires and barbecues on Guy Fawkes night, cricket matches and country dances, church bazaars and anything else they could think of. But the Family went, as such old families too often do, the parish acquired the green and the parish council put an end to the popular junketing. There was such a horrid mess afterwards and the bonfires burned the grass, it said, it really looked like a battlefield or a tinker settlement. It could not have done so for long, as volunteers were always ready to clear things up, but there is no arguing with Jacks in office. They even tried, apparently, to stop the Hunts from meeting on it, an ideal spot for the purpose and handy for their stirrup-cups from the Swan, but here at least they met their match; and the Morris Dancers still give a display in the grounds of the Swan itself from time to time, before an appreciative audience collected outside on the green. But with the onward march of democracy the village people no longer had any public space to call their own, and most of the old merry-making died away. Now the grass is nicely trimmed, and a few boys kicking a ball about or a lady making a sketch of the pond are the only signs of life upon it.

Another mourned the passing of institutions, such as are disappearing all over the country. The village bobby, for instance, who had known everyone all his life, who looked the other way if a poor man was taking a pheasant home to his family, and who could clout a young offender without fear of prosecution by an irate parent – that friendly calming presence has gone. Squad cars patrol, and come out fast enough if needed, but the crews are often from other parts, without any particular knowledge of local affairs. I could not see that this mattered much, as there seemed to be no crime in the village at all; but perhaps the speaker, a publican, was embittered by the all-out war against drinking drivers, which has had the effect of frightening perfectly respectable people away from the inns.

A mother lamented that so little was done to entertain the young nowadays and keep them at home. It was nobody's fault, she said: people had tried to start things often enough but as soon as they got them going the motorbike boys moved in from outside and there was trouble. Those youths are indeed a fearsome lot, thundering through the quiet land on their Hondas and Toyamas with the speed and racket of the new fighter planes that hurtle across the sky overhead: they seem to require noise to assure themselves of being alive, and have such a name for that and aggro of one kind or another that certain pubs will not serve them or only in one segregated room.

Others, younger still, had a pastime that I never came across before. They would get into the one and only public telephone and hold interminable conversations with some one who wasn't there. Fuming outside, I have watched the little devils at it: no money went into the box but on and on they babbled, deriving a voluptuous glee from the annoyance of the would-be caller.

'But they are not our kids,' the village people said emphatically. They came from the Holiday Centre up the road that was such a thorn in the local flesh.

One rainy day after a monologue had lasted twenty minutes or so, I pushed the door open and confronted the brat who was delivering it. 'What's the idea?' I demanded. 'You aren't talking to anyone.'

175

'Yus, I fuckin am,' was the prompt reply. 'I'm fuckin on to me fuckin fambly.'

'Are you from the Home?'

'Wot if I fuckin am? It's no fuckin business of yours. Ullo, ma? ma? Sorry about that hinterruption,' she cooed down the line.

Plainly, an artist of a kind.

These monkeys made short work of the directories as well, tearing them up with the thoroughness of an office shredder. I stopped a Telecom van on the road one day and asked the driver to supply a new one.

'Well, all right,' he said doubtfully. 'But it won't be new for long. Not normally. We normally put one in every month, and normally the kids have it to bits in a couple of days.'

It was a peculiar concept of normality.

Certainly at times one caught the jungle noises of the city here, almost indeed felt the scorching breath of its feral inhabitants on one's neck. One night that I was on a late visit, the company was startled by a series of bloodcurdling yells and whoops as of Indians on the warpath. The pubs were just closing, and we expected that this hullabaloo would be followed by another, of motorbikes roaring up to Malvern. But no, it went on and grew worse, moving slowly in our direction: evidently these Mohicans, if such they were, were on foot. In front of the house I was in, they stopped and treated us to a little serenade, a medley of Pop, catcalls and bursts of manic laughter. One of our party stole out through the darkness and came back with the news that all was well, it was only staff from the Holiday Centre, 'monitors' as they were laughingly called, enjoying their well-earned relaxation.

The two local public houses were anything but disorderly, however. Both were well-conducted and people left quietly and promptly at the proper time, whatever they did outside. Only once have I heard the closing bell rung twice and I regret to say that it was tolling for myself and two friends, who had got carried away in discussion. Both places were attractive in different ways, the Swan with the advantage of its beautiful location, and plenty of room in the garden for sitting out and enjoying the scene, the Ewe and Lamb with a great deal of atmosphere and rather more of the old pub spirit. You constantly saw new faces at the Swan, people from outside who tended to come in groups and keep to themselves, whereas the Ewe had a core of regulars, local countrymen with good Worcestershire voices, who would easily accept a stranger and draw him into their lively, often ribald, talk. I have had much entertainment in merely listening to their subversive comments on life, political corruption in high places, fiddles everywhere – even the football pools were assumed to be rigged in some diabolical way – skulduggery in the racing world, the police, local government, and the foolishness of what used to be called the upper classes.

One of them was a real specialist in this particular field and would reproduce the inane remarks he claimed to have heard in a faultlessly posh accent. He once recounted how a woman who employed him, and whom I happened to know, had said that a certain ladder would be too short to reach the roof; whereupon he had gravely suggested cutting a few rungs off the bottom and lashing them on to the top. 'What a marvellous idea!' he quoted her as saying: 'I nevah thought of that!' Unless she was pulling his leg as well, she had said nothing of the kind, but he had her voice and diction to the life, and was gleefully applauded by everyone present.

I was particularly interested in his performances, as they exposed a fallacy that my generation had rubbed into it from childhood, namely, that working-class people spoke as they did because they knew no better, not having enjoyed our advantages. I had long had doubts of this because they all read to some extent, if only the sporting page of the Daily Mirror, and they all listened to the wireless or tele, and yet they went through life cheerfully making every possible mistake of grammar and pronunciation because they jolly well chose to. It was simply due to the English dislike of their betters, or rather, their sturdy conviction that no such beings existed, and as for our 'advantages', we could keep them.

'Educated idiots, that's what they are,' the thinker concluded, complacently.

'But can idiots be educated?' I asked in a spirit of mischief.

'Course they can, that's 'ow they got where they are, like I said.'

177

Here he was reproved by another of the assembly, who prided himself on a knowledge of etiquette. 'That's no flippin way to speak to a flippin lady,' he observed.

'I didn't mean 'er,' the thinker protested. 'I never. No offence, mate, 'ere, drink that off and 'ave another.'

Goodness knew what the honest fellow meant, but he was very good company.

Their class attitudes were interesting too, because on the whole they were the same as in the days of my youth, when they really had much to grouse about. Thirty shillings still bought a certain amount then, but it was hardly enough to bring up a family. Now these same people had cars, colour television, subsidies for their children, holidays abroad, but they clung to their old sense of being exploited in some nefarious way, and generally downtrodden by the grasping bourgeoisie.

Few if any of them worked on the land, although they were good countrymen who shot, fished, went ferreting, raised their own vegetables, knew where the nuts, crab apples and mushrooms were best and what the weather was going to do. Mostly they were wage-earners, a kind of rustic proletariat, building, road-mending, lorry-driving, or employed by the Water Board. There was one snooty middle-class pair, married, who came in every day, downed a few gins and left again without uttering a single word to each other or anyone else; and a commercial traveller, who held forth tirelessly on the topics of the day by virtue of his superior culture, and was a favourite joke in his absence.

One morning two strangers walked in, smartish middle-aged men with a towny look about them, and the usual game began of trying to find out what they were up to without any direct questions being asked. This seemed to amuse them very much and presently one of them smilingly invited us all to guess at their occupation. Reps, thought some, turf accountants, thought others, but no. From the county offices? Surveyors? No, no. I wondered if they were plain clothes police or dealing in secondhand cars, but kept these conjectures to myself. Finally, they consented to tell us – they were farmers, looking for something to buy in the neighbourhood.

178

Farmers! They looked as if they had never walked across a field in their buckled suede shoes, or held a sample of wheat in their smooth white hands: they must be the new businesslike breed that tore hedges down, sprayed the weeds, poisoned the birds, drove away the little wild creatures, built hideous animal factories – and they were coming here, like some Egyptian plague!

It was a gruesome idea, but the locals made short work of it. No sooner had the 'farmers' driven off in their glossy Cortina than they were taken to pieces with a will. It was generally agreed that it was a con (like everything else), the men were tinkers, gypsies even, prospecting for scrap metal or similar loot; someone swore he had seen them prowling over the nearby rubbish tip, another recalled their being requested to leave The Drum and Monkey, while a third had read in the paper that two men of their description were being sought by the police to help in some inquiry.

This character assassination was performed without malice, indeed, with much good humour and mirth. I felt that never before had I met such a concentration of agreeable human wickedness as in that simple pub. Set in the very heart of noble Hanley Swan, with a flood of good will and good works rolling all around, it held on its way like some incorruptible Ark and, for me, put a piquant finishing touch to this most appealing of villages.

Chapter Nineteen

Now it was time to pack and leave, partly because money was running out, a perverse little habit it has, and partly because a friend from Spain had proposed himself for a stay on Achill. Things were boiling up for the summer holidays in general and, rather than face the rigours of the Irish Mail, I decided to fly from Birmingham, which involved passing through the city itself, indeed spending some hours there, en route for the airport. As if to ease the pain of departure for me, Brum was quite especially horrible that day: it was hard to realize that all the quiet lovely places I had seen were but a short distance off.

As for the people, they seemed to belong, in fact they did, to another world. In the Bull Ring, where only a sprinkling of English faces were to be seen, a black youth tried to seize my handbag, unsuccessfully true, but none of the passersby took any notice whatever. Another inter-racial incident struck a merrier note: there was a Ladies cloakroom describing itself as de luxe, charging ten whole pence instead of two and, curious to see what the luxury consisted of, I slipped in a coin. Hovering near, evidently awaiting her chance, was a gigantic negress who made a spirited attempt to squeeze in with me; but I was too quick for her and she was left outside, raining blows on the door and protesting loudly against the injustice. The cloakroom was the standard thing, but clean and tidy, which must have been what the notice had in mind; and on leaving I smartly pulled the door to, frustrating a second try and provoking another burst of recrimination.

These recollections faded completely once we were in the air, with the green hills and valleys and woods spread out below us, bathed in the warm glow of the evening sun. Presently the calm blue sea appeared with its edging of white foam and the fishing smacks making for harbour, like so many little brown butterflies. Everything spoke of peace and order and happiness: one knew from reading the newspapers, including my own contributions, that this was nonsense, that everything was as bad as possible, except that it would shortly be worse, and nothing lay ahead but decline and decay; but what one 'knows' from sources of that kind and what one feels in one's bones are a different affair. I was in a state of tranquil elation as things were; but had I been able to see into the future, to realize that in a very few months the unhoped-for would happen, that someone would make an unhoped-for offer for my house and enable me to return to England for good, I might well have exploded for joy.